There's a Better Way to Lose Weight than Ordinary Dieting— This Is It! FASTING

It's *not* starving. In fact, it's a whole lot easier to achieve weight loss this way than with prolonged low-calorie diets. Once the decision has been made and the fast begun, a feeling of well-being sets in, and the result is a comfortable and sane weight loss. All you need is your doctor's permission and you're on your way to the slimmer, trimmer, healthier *you* you've always wanted. And don't forget: FASTING IS FUN!

SHIRLEY ROSS is the author of *The Interior Ecology Cookbook*, *Plant Consciousness*, *Plant Care*, and *Nature's Drinks*.

DR. ELLIOTT J. HOWARD is a Fellow of the American College of Physicians, Fellow of the American College of Cardiology, Medical Director of the Foundation for the Study of Exercise, Stress, and Heart, and Associate Medical Director of Cardiometrics

Books by Shirley Ross:

THE INTERIOR ECOLOGY COOKBOOK

PLANT CONSCIOUSNESS, PLANT CARE

NATURE'S DRINKS

FASTING:
The Super Diet

by Shirley Ross

Foreword by
Elliott J. Howard, M.D., F.A.C.P.

BALLANTINE BOOKS • NEW YORK

All rights reserved. For information write St. Martin's Press,
New York, N.Y. 10010. Published in the United States by
Ballantine Books, a division of Random House, Inc., New
York, and simultaneously in Canada by Ballantine Books of
Canada Ltd., Toronto, Canada.

Library of Congress Catalog Card Number: 75-34345

ISBN 0-345-25090-7-175

This edition published by arrangement with St. Martin's Press

Manufactured in the United States of America

First Ballantine Books Edition: June, 1976

Note

Fasting has had good results in aiding weight loss as well as in alleviating mental and physical problems. However, nothing in this book should be regarded as medical advice or treatment. Since individuals respond to change in their diet in ways determined by their particular constitutions, no one should undertake a fast—or any diet—without the advice and close supervision of his or her physician throughout the fast and the period of readjustment which follows it.

To Gerard Dombrowski and Harold M. Wit

ACKNOWLEDGMENTS

Several people generously contributed their time and information towards the making of this book. I wish to thank the following people: Damian Bisch, Gerard Dombrowski, R. N., Elliott J. Howard, M. D., Danny Hughes, Tony King, Phyllis Levine, Katinka Matson, Professor Elaine Pagels, Michael Perkins, David Sarlin, Dr. Edwin Schlossberg, Valerie Wade, David and Jo Ann Weinrib, Harold M. Wit, and Dr. D. D. Zettel. A special note of thanks goes to my agent, John Brockman, and my editor, Tom Dunne.

TABLE OF CONTENTS

Foreword

by Elliott J. Howard, M.D.; Fellow of the American College of Physicians; Fellow of the American College of Cardiology, Medical Director of the Foundation for the Study of Exercise, Stress and the Heart; Associate Medical Director of Cardiometrics.

FASTING, THE COMPLETE abstention from food consumption, might seem at first thought to be a drastic and grossly unnatural thing to do. Yet there is a long and fascinating history of traditional fasting which is associated with remarkable psychological and physical effects. Fasting had an important part in inducing the spiritual effects of ancient holy rituals. Religious and moral orders used fasting to facilitate the abstention from evil and communication with God. Fasting began the anti-sensuality movement, the mortification of the flesh.

Currently, fasting is not simply another fad for a quick weight loss schema, but rather it has a definite place in the life-long effort for weight control, and is especially useful for the obese individual. The vast majority of present-day Americans and Europeans (the regions of plenty in the modern world) have an over-riding lack of control over their dietary habits, a characteristic which pervades societies as they become part of "progressive civilizations" and more and more of their numbers are uncontrollably overweight. As a result, the most confounded ideas for weight loss can be sold to the public, the more gimmicky, the more easily sold. The only "normal" right way for an otherwise normal but overweight person to lose weight is by a well-balanced, lower caloric, prolonged diet, but this is the least utilized diet because it requires constant personal effort and triumph over moment-to-moment temptation. Fasting is the ultimate triumph, but in fact is considerably easier to achieve than the prolonged lower calorie diet because once the mental confrontation has been made, the decision made, and the fast begun, a euphoric condition "sets in" along with a pleasant sense of mystical communication, which places the "faster" apart from the ordinary over-eating public. Assuming medical clearance from contra-indicating metabolic ills, the fast is a safe and sane method of weight loss. To be sure, the aftermath when the faster returns to food consumption may be fraught with psychological hazards, but with self-control and/or a little psychological guidance and support, a steady-state can be achieved and the goals maintained.

Fasting cannot be used as a fad to get something quick and easy, because it is neither quick nor easy. It must be a complete facing-up to one's own psychological weakness and a determination to succeed in mastering one's will; otherwise, at the end of the fast, all controls are lost in favor of the "rewards" one has earned. If one can succeed in this triumph for periods of four to ten days, one can retrain his or her permanent routine eating habits. Occasionally, longer periods up to thirty days may be necessary to achieve certain special goals.

In this well-researched book, Shirley Ross has intelligently brought together all the available scientific and biological data as well as the ancient and current spiritual experiences inherent in fasting. One can learn the nature of fasting, be it for massive weight loss, periodic weight control, or ritual spiritual communicative techniques.

As a physician, I acknowledge that there is still much controversy attached to some of the ideas expressed here, and it is not my intent to endorse as beneficial the ritualistic ideas of ancient or current cultures or cults. However, I can support the safety (with certain limitations), the effectiveness, the psychological benefits of facing one's weakness and overcoming the day-to-day temptations of poor and excessive eating habits. I can confirm the unexpected mood elevating influence of the euphoric sensations which accompany fasting.

There are certain serious patho-physiologic events which may occur in the body, requiring the attention and correction by a physician. Thus, a prolonged period of fasting (more than one week) ought to have the attention of an interested physician. People with certain metabolic conditions ought not to engage in fasting or at least not without special medical attention.

Fasting is not for everyone, but if there is no contra-indication and this is the way you choose for yourself, this book will introduce you to a special medium.

"Fasting possesses great power. If practiced with the right intention, it makes man a friend of God. The demons are aware of that."

—TERTULLIAN

"In general he condemned all things alien to the gods inasmuch as they lead us away from the association with the gods. . . . Whatever was an obstacle to mantic activity, or to the clearness and purity of the soul, or to the state of moderation and virtue, this he recommended avoiding. And he did not approve of things which were opposed to clarity and soiled the remaining clearness of the soul and the phantasms of sleep. This he ordained concerning food in general."

—IAMBLICHUS, on Pythagoras

"Fasting is better than prayer."
—ST. CLEMENT

Introduction

"*Many more days went by, however, and that too came to an end. An overseer's eye fell on the cage one day and he asked the attendants why this perfectly good cage should be left standing there unused with dirty straw inside it; nobody knew, until one man, helped out by the notice board, remembered about the hunger artist. They poked into the straw with sticks and found him in it. 'Are you still fasting?' asked the overseer. 'When on earth do you mean to stop?' 'Forgive me, everybody,' whispered the hunger artist. Only the overseer, who had his ears to the bars, understood him. 'Of course,' said the overseer, and tapped his head with a forefinger to let the attendants know what state the man was in, 'we forgive you.' 'I always wanted you to admire my fasting,' said the hunger artist. 'We do admire it,' said the overseer, affably. 'But you shouldn't admire it,' said the hunger artist. 'Well then we don't admire it,' said the overseer, 'but why shouldn't we admire it?' 'Because I have to fast, I can't help it,' said the hunger artist. 'What a fellow you are,' said the overseer, 'and why can't you help it?' 'Because,' said the hunger artist, lifting his head a little and speaking, with his lips pursed, as if for a kiss, right into the overseer's ear, so that no syllable might be lost, 'because I couldn't find the food I liked. If I had found it, believe me, I should have made no fuss and stuffed myself like you or anyone else.' These were his last words, but in his dimming eyes remained the firm though no longer proud persuasion that he was still continuing to fast."*

FRANZ KAFKA, "A Hunger Artist"

FRANZ KAFKA, in his story, "A Hunger Artist," laments, "Just try to explain to anyone the art of fasting! Anyone who has no feeling for it cannot be made to understand it." Perhaps the only way to feel it, to understand it, is to do it. This book is filled with practical information on how people have successfully conducted short- and long-term fasts. It's not necessarily that simple.

Shortly after reading "A Hunger Artist" many years ago, I became infatuated with the idea of doing a fast, so much so, that upon completion of the story I simply stopped eating and in a period of twenty-four hours, with nothing to guide me but my own inexperience and uncommonly bad sense, I embarked on a definitive course on "how not to be a hunger artist."

First, in order to lose a few pounds, I thought I would also not drink liquids to any great degree. This, of course, leads to dehydration and can cause very serious complications. Second, I had a full schedule of work and social activities. Third, I decided that it would be nice to have a steam bath, so I went to my health club and spent almost an hour in the sauna, not being aware that fasting leads to abnormally low blood pressure (postural hypotension) and that the effect of hot baths, especially something like a steam bath, leads to dizziness and fainting spells. I literally flew out of the health club and started to walk, rather "fly" down Fifty-seventh Street in New York. It was night. The bright lights in Times Square, as I turned down Seventh Avenue were unreal. They glowed in a way I had never seen before, they danced, they did tricks on my eyes. I walked down the avenue. My feet were doing one step at a time, but I felt as though I were three feet off the ground, powered by no mechanical means other than a great rush of energy. I began to sense that I was totally out of my skull. The high was very euphoric, but I knew I was out of control. I began to get very dizzy, and grabbed a lamppost for dear life. I made my way very slowly into a hotel, totally paranoid that everyone in the lobby was staring at me, and called a friend who was equally ignorant about fasting. She said, "You need to eat, right away." Eat. Sure. When I walked out of the hotel lobby, standing straight in front of me was the legendary Stage Delicatessen. "Chicken soup" flashed in my head. Break the fast with chicken soup. I went in, sat down, acting as cool as possible under the circumstances, and started to order chicken soup when the waiter shoved a menu under my nose and said, "Eat, enjoy . . . you're too skinny." "Food," I thought, "mmmm." My chicken soup arrived, then my three-decker pastrami, corned beef, and turkey (with cole slaw and Russian dressing), then the side order of potato pancakes. I ate, and ate. I ate some more. Within minutes the dizziness passed, I came back down to planet earth and found myself stuffing my face in the Stage Delicatessen. I thought the whole process was completed. I made my way home and went to sleep. About two hours later I awoke in the greatest pain I had ever, or have ever since, experienced. It was as though my whole intestine was coming apart. I thought I was going to die. It was 2:00 A.M., and I just lay there in agony for two hours until, finally, the pain subsided. Luckily, I awoke the next day with no ill effects. I had a new determination to learn everything I could about fasting, realizing that without knowing even the basics, a fast of very short duration, if improperly conducted, could be a very scary and painful experience. I would yet be "a hunger artist."

Soon after this first attempt at fasting, I moved to California and became involved in founding what was soon to be a famous health food restaurant in Los Angeles, H.E.L.P. (for Health, Education, Love, and Peace). During this experience I became increasingly aware of the relationship between food and my body. Yet I wanted to go further. I wanted to see the effect of not eating, of total food withdrawal. At the time I belonged to a meditation group under the leadership of a "mystical" teacher, and I gradually learned about and got into fasting . . . the correct way. What I learned from these experiences, my subsequent fasts, and extensive research on the subject, is the basis for my interest in writing this book and sharing the information with you.

How much can you say about not eating? I have found that most of my knowledge of fasting when I first got started was from friends and teachers. The available literature was not very useful. Many of the books currently on the market were either written fifty years ago, or based on conceptions of that era. In almost all cases, the medical terminology is totally out of date and as if it were taken from a time capsule. Some of the concepts are little changed from those used by the ancient Greeks. While many of the theories sound appealing, there is little scientific backing for them. Some of these books are not only misleading, they can be dangerous as well.

There is an interesting situation at work in the area of fasting. The "natural health"-oriented people advocate fasting as a cure-all for any and all ailments. You name it, and they will print a case study of a miracle cure induced through a fast. On the other hand, medical doctors have little interest or understanding in the finer points of fasting, even though the practice is now widely prescribed for cases of chronic obesity. This later area has provided a wealth of raw data on the physiology of fasting during the last fifteen years.

For the first time, thanks to recent research, we know what happens to the body during a fast. It's not simple. The body is a complex organism. More important, the methods of studying and knowing the body have changed. The old "mechanical" body is out. In its place is a far more complex and sophisticated systems approach. There are no longer easy answers and explanations. "This" does not cause "that." Millions of subtle interactions take place every second, and the determinations we can make are studies of the state of the system at any given point in time.

What this means to you, if you are considering going on a fast, is that (1) most of the books currently in print on fasting are hopelessly dated, and (2) medical people, while they have the research and information, do not have the broader picture necessary to fully appreciate the very valid and important benefits of fasting.

There are many ways to know and experience the subject of fasting. You can investigate doctor's test tubes and find the microscopic realities invisible to the naked eye; you can go and live briefly in the past, fasting through the eyes of the ancients in a quest for spiritual development; you can study the clinical results of medically supervised weight-reduction fasts; you can look at the mythology of early twentieth-century fasting proponents; you can get inside the heads of interesting contemporary individuals as they fast and begin to feel their firsthand experience; you can try your own fast and reexamine your relationship to food and what it means to you.

For myself, personal experience has always been the most interesting of the above methods. I am thin, so I have no need to lose weight. I eat well and take care of myself. I don't need to fast to gain good health, nor do I believe that fasting should be presented and sold to people as some kind of cure. I have written two other books in this general area, both dealing with food; *The Interior Ecology Cookbook,* Straight Arrow, 1970, and *Nature's Drinks, Vintage,* 1973, explored the benefits of using proper foods and raw juices, respectively. I believe that this book on fasting goes one step further.

I hope you will use this book to gain a better understanding of that complex and amazing process we are now beginning to call *bodymind.* I have tried to let fasters and the facts speak for themselves. Whether you decide to fast or not is a decision that you, in consultation with your doctor, should make. If you decide to fast, I sincerely hope that the information provided in this book will help you toward a fulfilling and healthful experience.

1

FASTING
IN ANTIQUITY

ONLY IN THE past decade have we begun to unravel the mysteries of the precise biochemical and physiological changes that occur in our bodies and brains when we fast. There is now an explanation for the metabolic functions of the brain which, during fasting, produce visions, hallucinations, special clarity, and euphoria.

The ancients did not have the benefits of modern science to explain their own experiences. But they hardly needed it. Through their rituals and everyday practice, fasting was the ultimate high, the "drug" of antiquity. Plato. Pythagoras. Abraham. Mohammed. Jesus. Our greatest religious and philosophical teachers all knew the mysteries and ancient secrets of the fast.

Fasting is power. Fasting is magic. A communication with the holy. A trip through space and time. The past, present, future blended into a divine contact with true ecstasy of life. Fasting reveals the godlike nature in man. It dissolves the rational, the sane mind which lives by established rules and procedures. Plato points out that there are two minds: the rational mind, and one brought forth out of the latter by fasting. This is a new, prophetic space, an ecstatic, mindless space in which one can find seclusion in order to prepare for divine and holy dreams. According to Plato, such a state is artless and unlearnable, and accessible only through abstinence from food.

Fasting is a common denominator for virtually every religion in every part of the world. It appears in various places in various guises with seemingly no connection. In New Guinea, year-long partial abstentions from food are practiced by boys. Students in India fast before starting a new course of study. In Central Brazil, both wife and husband fast at times during pregnancy. The Eskimos and North American Indians must fast before ordination to the priesthood. Peruvians fast as penance for sexual misdeeds. The instances are as many as there are cultures in the world.

In Islam, the following situations call for fasting: before entering a sanctuary; before a sacrifice; at transition to a new stage in life; at ordination; after a death; before prayer; when seeking revenge; to induce dreams, visions, oracles; during illness; to atone for sins; as a good work; as part of asceticism; as a periodic ritual; in case of impending natural disasters; in case of war or other calamities; while sowing or plowing; at harvest time; at the sidereal New Year.[1]

Many of these rites of passage deal with death and rebirth. The main point is to ritualize various aspects of life. Life is not taken simply for what it is; without these rites there is in fact no life. Renewal and appropriation of power are sought. In that sense fasting, besides being an indication of death, is also purifying. It clears the way for new life.

Fasting for Supernatural Power

Food contains supernatural powers. It is to be both desired and feared. Indeed, "with primitive ancient religion an important meaning of fasting may be found. This lies in the animistic-dynamistic concepts relating to food. Food is presumed to contain 'supernatural' power which actually turns all eating and drinking into a sacramental act. This power is necessary for life, and is therefore desirable, but it may also be dangerous. This means that the partaking of food always binds one in a supernatural way. Thus the magical potion binds to the one who prepares it and thus also the communal meal binds those who partake of it to each other. It is clear that here the meaning of fasting is a tabu inherent in the food itself. The divine power of food, present to an exceptional degree in new food, is dangerous when eaten at the wrong time or mixed with food from an earlier period. By fasting at this time one purifies oneself and prepares oneself for the consumption of new, sacred food." [2]

The pagan fasted "to endow him with the extraordinary, superhuman powers required in preparation for magical intercouse with supernatural forces. The magic papyri, for instance, lay the greatest stress on the ritual purity of the magician, his assistants, and mediums, and promises success only if the magic action is performed in this state. The prescriptions dealing with ritual purity in magic usually require a longer or shorter period of complete or partial abstention." [3]

Fasting for Sanctification of the Body

Chrysostom, patriarch of Constantinople (A.D. 400): "Of the things that enter the stomach, not all are turned into nourishment, for not all of the food itself is nutritious, but part of it in the process of digestion is turned into nourishment and the rest into the stool. . . . Now if food be taken in too great a quantity, even the nutritive part can be harmful . . . for when gluttony, like a rain-storm, has flooded the intestines, it throws everything into a turmoil, and it makes organs that up till then had been quiet and healthy drift sluggishly on the surface. . . . So physicians tell us that want is the mother of health." [4]

Consider the wisdom of Athenaeus, a Greek physician in Rome (A.D. 50) who asks us to look at "the effects of fasting: it cures diseases, dries up bodily

humors, puts demons to flight, gets rid of impure
thoughts, makes the mind clearer and the heart purer,
the body sanctified, and raises man to the throne of
God."

The general conclusion of the Greeks was that the
fast has two main beneficial effects. First, it divorces
the mind from the body. The soul escapes from the
heavy flesh and rises gently to the gods. Second, the
mind is free of "the fumes" of food, which are a source
of confusion and darkness. This attitude is exemplified
by a dialogue written by St. Gregory of Nazianzuz,
Christian Bishop in Asia Minor (A.D. 330–395):

> *Pneuma:* But my pleasure is to have no pleas-
> ure, not to have my body swollen with things fill-
> ing it inside, sick with the infirmity of the
> unhealthy, breathing from my throat the sickly,
> sweet odor of filth, constraining my mind with the
> weight of my fat.
> *Kosmos:* For me the sweetmeats!
> *Pneuma:* Bread is my condiment, and my drink
> pure water, surpassing sweet.[5]

Pursuant to the dualism of body and mind, Clement
of Alexandria, a Greek theologian and writer (A.D.
150–215) believed that fasting empties the soul of
matter, and clears the soul and the body, readying
both for revelation. For him the only true food was
"this present life." Basil the Great, the bishop of
Caesarea in Asia Minor (A.D. 329–379), quotes
Pythagoras as asking, "Why don't you stop making
a prison of your body?" Of cooked food, he deplor-
ingly notes, "The smoking fumes, as it were, of rich
and plentiful food, ascending, cut off like a thick cloud
the illuminations of the Holy Spirit which are infused
in the mind."

The prevalent belief of the ancient Greeks was that
the soul reached its greatest power when totally cut off
from the lower digestive activity of the body. The fast
freed the soul from the influence of the body. The soul

entered higher worlds nearer to the gods, a better place to directly receive their messages.

Fasting to Understand the Nature of Hidden Things

A story is told of Daniel, who fasted for three days to gain better understanding of the dream of the King of Babylon. None of the courtiers believed man could see into the future. Daniel, fasting along with prayer, knew that God would appear with the answer.

Daniel was a vegetarian, known for his beautiful body and cultured mind. God gave Daniel wisdom, vision, and insights. He knew the true nature of things. He understood the meaning of life and of God. Through his fasting he expected to receive the hidden meanings of things from the angel of God. Tertullian, a fifth-century Roman writer, reports, "I, Daniel, was mourning for three weeks. I ate no pleasant bread; meat and wine did not enter my mouth; I was not anointed with oil until the three weeks had passed." Enter God's Angel: "Daniel, you are a man deserving pity, fear not: for from the first day on which you gave your soul to meditation and humiliation before God, your word has been heard, and I have come because of your word."

Fasting for Prophecy

Pythagoras, the great Greek philosopher and mathematician (582–500 B.C.), would not eat beans, because this particular food caused flatulence and bad dreams. The gods revealed their higher truths to him while he slept. Thus the pagans always went through a preparatory period including a fast to prepare themselves for dream-oracles. They did not think of dreams as being subjective, but as objective reports of things to come. The fast allowed the dreamers to purify their bodies and souls and to prepare for the direct communication.

Fasting was a major tool of the pagan prophets, [those who claimed to see the future]. The fast brought with it magical powers. The magicians prepared for prophecy by repeating the following prayer seven times: "Let me know beforehand the near and distant, and the past, all that happened today, once and for all." [6]

Fast, the ancients believed, and you would become an oracle. Pythagoras: "If you are pure, I will bestow upon you the gift of foreknowledge, and fill your eyes with brightness so that you will distinguish a god, recognize a hero, and put to shame shadowy phantoms when they practice deception by assuming the form of man." He above all believed that in addition to leading to scientific skills and power of prophecy, fasting would enable one to achieve true divine knowledge, and not just opinions regarding the gods. Pythagoras left the real day-to-day world and fasted his way into a divine state. Many believe that his fasting practices generated the insight necessary for his incredibly elegant mathematical theories, a system of thought that survives to this modern day.

Fasting to Be as God

Prophyrius, a Greek philosopher, explains that the neo-Platonic philosophers had a goal to make themselves as close to the image of the gods as possible. The gods were without wants and desires. This was one of their major characteristics. For man to fast, to abstain from food, was to approach the godlike state. He further believed that while food was beneficial for the body, it left the soul to perish.

Fasting to Find God

Whenever fasting appeared in ancient times, it re-established contact with the holy, a communication that is a matter of life and death for the religious man.

For primitive man, the fast was direct communication, his entry into the realm of the spirit. His gods lived in this realm and could be reached through the practices of the fast. The primitive fasted to improve perception or to prepare for revelations. His goal was ecstasy.

Later, Jewish and Christian practices introduced ethics and morality to the fast. Daniel fasted not to gain ecstasy but to humble himself before God, who could mediate his journeys to the privileged space. The ritual fast was no longer directly beneficial, but an ethical religious act. It was an abstinence from evil, an attitude of the mind in front of God.

Christian fasting practices developed even though Jesus left no laws on the subject. He did, it is known, undertake severe fasts himself and recommended the practice, along with prayer, as a cure for persons possessed of the devil.

During the first five centuries of Christianity, fasting was no longer purely an ascetic act. Men now fasted to find in themselves virtues that God wanted them to possess. Around the fourth century A.D., the Church began to ritualize the fast in order to curb the over-zealousness of individual ascetics. Through various rituals they created a corporate practice under which personal asceticism was brought under the canopy of the Church.

Still, asceticism was not that easily renounced, as is shown in the following passage from "The Apocalypse of Baruch": "The prophet is directed to keep in his heart whatever God commands him and to enclose it in the innermost part of his mind. Then God will show him His mighty judgment and unsearchable ways. The prophet is ordered to sanctify himself, eating no bread, drinking no water, and speaks to nobody. Then he is to come back and God will reveal himself to him, conversing with him about things which are true and giving him information about the certain occurrence of future events. The prophet sanctifies himself in the way commanded by God." [7]

The ritual fasts are ascetic reinterpretations of those of primitive man. They were "initially developed from many centuries side by side with ascetic fasting, so that extended collective and periodic periods of fasting arise. One can here point to the later Jewish practice of partial fasting for forty days before the day of atonement, i.e. the month of Elul and the first days of Tishri, the practice of Christians since Nicea of partial fasting for forty days before Easter, as well as forty days before Christmas; the Manichean fast of one month before the Bema festival; and the Muslim practice of partial fasting not only in Ramadan but also the two preceeding months. Although, except for the Muslim fast, all these extended periods of fast are formally connected with particular festivals." [8]

Fasting with the Ancients

Can it be that we have something to learn from the ancients? Perhaps they were trying to bridge the gap of the time and space to leave their own messages with us. Finally, these words from A.D. 150 by Hermes in "The Shepherd:" "When you are going to fast, observe it in this way: first, avoid any evil and desire, and purify your heart of all the vain things in the world. Your fast will be perfect if you do this. And this is the way you should eat: after fulfilling all you are supposed to do on your fast day, then eat nothing but bread and water, and of the food which you were going to eat, measure out the same quantity and give this to a widow or orphan or other needy person."

Notes

[1] K. Wagtendock, *Fasting in the Koran,* Leiden: E. J. Brill, 1968.

[2] Wagtendock, op. cit.

[3] Rudolph Arbessman, O.S.A. "Fasting and Prophecy in Pagan and Christian Antiquity." Traditio Vol. 7 1949–51. New York: Fordham University Press.

[4] Herbert Musurillo, *The Problem of Ascetical Fasting in the Greek Patristic Writers,* New York: Fordham University Press, 1956.

[5] Musurillo, op. cit.

[6] Arbessman, op. cit.

[7] Arbessman, op. cit.

[8] Wagtendock, op. cit.

2

STORY OF A FIFTY-SEVEN-DAY FAST

"For what can be more efficacious than fasting? By observing it, we come nearer to God, resist the devil, and overcome the enticement of vices. Fasting has always been the food of virtue. Abstinence is the source of chaste thoughts, rational aspirations, and sound counsels. Through hardships endured of our own accord, the unlawful desires of the flesh are extinguished, and new life is installed into our virtues."

—St. Leo

David is a thirty-year-old inventor and computer expert who lives in San Francisco and the Santa Cruz Mountains:

It was mostly a question of curiosity. I decided to try not eating and see what it felt like. I knew that nothing seriously wrong could come from it, so I went for four days without eating. I found that I didn't drink enough water, and at times I was terribly dehydrated, so I called that off. After that I didn't feel any overwhelming desire to fast for a long period of time.

A year or so later I was graduating from college and tried fasting again. This time it was for about ten days. The experience was about the same, as it took about three or four days before any form of hunger went away, and I remember drinking coffee during that time, which quelled a lot of hunger pains. But I didn't find it terribly painful to go through at all, and found it quite pleasant afterward. I remember noticing that half the stores in the city were devoted to purveying food in one form or another. It gave me a chance to examine my own relationship with food without hunger being a factor, because there was no hunger whatsoever after I had adjusted to not eating. The ease with which my stomach adjusted to not eating seemed to indicate to me that this is the body's own mode of living during what must have been hard times. During such times, people must have been nomadic and food consisted of catching a deer once a week or once a month and it eventually spoiled and you didn't even have fire. You would eat what you could right there and then, fill your belly, and then by the time you found something else it might be completely empty. At that time I realized that if this was the case, we are animals and cannot be expected to have a regular food supply, and this means that fat has its place in our scheme of things. After all, the body is a very efficient user of biological chemicals and things like that and fat itself is possibly the single most common and usable source of food for the body, because the body has stored it and knows how to use it. It didn't store it for antiaesthetic reasons . . . but as a means of retaining food you will need before you find the next antelope or the next harvest. The weight that accumulates on your body is to accumulate in places that are out of the way. Exercise reapportions fat and puts it in places where it doesn't get in the way. For instance, if you have fat around your legs and then start exercising your legs, you soon find that fat disappears from them, but is it because of the muscle exercise or because of some innate change that the body senses and says, "Hey, I'm this person, fat can't stay on this person's legs, because these legs are being used." It's nothing that conscious, but there's an adjusting mechanism that seems to work that way.

When I started my long fast, the circumstances were very much up in the air. I was alone for a period of a couple of weeks and planned to be alone in the fore-seeable future. I wanted some peace and time for re-flection. The Santa Cruz Mountains are quite beautiful, and the personal environment was very supportive. I was surrounded by friends in a community and there were no pressing or heavy demands—mental or physi-cal. I was developing certain technical products and inventions and had quite a bit of free time. I actually didn't have any intention of going on a marathon fast when I started.

A number of books recommended going from a meat diet to a vegetarian diet before fasting. They warn quite seriously about going from a meat diet into an extended fast. My preoccupation with fasting had to do with an interest in losing weight. I can't say exactly what percentage of motivation was the weight situa-tion, curiosity, or any other idea I had in my head at the time. There was some awareness on my part of the times when I had eaten only vegetables, and there was some change in my own consciousness due to what I ate . . . I was more aggressive and easier to anger.

Part of the pleasure of the fast came from the fact that in and around the Santa Cruz Mountains there is a loose-knit spiritually oriented community which fasts as part of yogic practice or their own interpretation of it. I was friendly with people in this community, al-though I never had shared their spiritual sensitivities. But through my fast I found myself sharing time and interests with these people . . . they became close friends and I found it very supportive. It was some-thing to talk about, something I was doing day in and day out. It had positive overtones for me, taking a step to reshaping my own body. I did want to lose some weight—I weighed 215 at the time, a bit too much even though I am 6′ 2″. During this period I wasn't into meditation. I knew about meditation on an intellectual level, but I wasn't consciously trying to meditate or pursue any spiritual path . . . it was me and my body and it was an experiment, just as much as trying out gourmet foods.

Fasting is being as intensely preoccupied with the lack of food as you might regularly be preoccupied with food. It's really a relationship with food and the metabolism of your own body. After the first three or four days, which I found very easy to go through, having gone through it a number of times before, hunger disappeared completely. During the first few days I drank a lot of liquids, and that tended to fill my stomach—coffee, bouillon, juices—but I didn't really feel hungry and this had to do with the excitement of beginning a new regimen. I stopped eating the morning of day one. It wasn't a question of having breakfast, but of deciding the night before that the next day might be a good day to start fasting and the day itself seemed propitious in the beginning. I don't remember taking any conscious steps to get all the food out of the house . . . it was more a natural orientation at the time.

I have dieted a number of different times on a number of different diets, and I believe that it is much easier to fast than to diet because dieting involves a constant interaction with food, much more so than fasting. Once you have been fasting for a while, it's dangerous to eat solid food. There's also some question of your stomach's ability to handle anything random that you might find attractive. You thus have to think twice before breaking it. It's a sense of commitment to yourself to continue a fast for a certain period.

At the commencement of my fast I started to sweat more and emitted rancid kinds of odors. I took showers more often and read a lot. I didn't do a lot of running socially, visiting people, etc., when I was starting, because there was a sort of continuing gnawing hunger.

It was somewhat intense in the first and second days, but there was no great crescendo, no feeling that it was going to peak and be overpowering or that I was going to fall down and be in overpowering pain, because I knew what to expect as I had done it before. I knew it just wouldn't happen.

The natural reaction to hunger is to eat. When you have the need to breathe, it means on the average that your body says this would be a good time to breathe right now, but you could hold your breath much longer, without physical damage to your body. I felt that my body would like to eat regularly; it's a nice thing to eat regularly; it's something the body is used to. I really tended to anthropomorphize—to ascribe a human form, in this case, to my stomach. I kept thinking that my stomach was getting pretty disgusted with me after the first ten days and saying, "Oh shit, you're not going to feed me, the hell with you," and then just closing up shop. It just gave up. It said, "Okay, I'm not going to get fed, so I'm closing up shop again, but in the meantime, I'm going to take a vacation." And I felt I didn't have any stomach. There were no sensations from my stomach region at all! There was no consciousness of a stomach! As a matter of fact, the feeling of being without a stomach made me feel very light . . . very, very light. I felt that I had a balloon inside me, more than anything else. And my mental state during the fast was continuously, immensely energetic, immensely alert, a very, very high state, very stimulated, as if you had stayed up all night in an exciting bull session. You're not as tired as that, just a sense of being elated by the intellectual context of what you're saying and what you feel, and I was definitely high during this time. I had read that it could be because of ketosis, but the effect was quite pleasant regardless of the cause. And it made me much more simpatico with the more spiritually oriented members of the community with whom I had established an acquaintance before. The acquaintance deepened into friendship because they had their own interpretations of why I was fasting. I certainly didn't know their specific appreciation of my situation, but I was enjoying it immensely: the conversation, the books they had which offered interpretations of what I was going through. Interestingly enough, a number of people I knew were encouraged to fast as a result of my fasting.

I think that thirty days was the longest that anyone fasted along with me. My brother came up for a while and fasted for fourteen days and enjoyed it, being carried along with the momentum of the thing. There was some context of mealtime . . . I did eat. This was not a water fast, a pure fast. I was into a variety of fruit and vegetable juices. There was a definite hierarchy of physical reactions to the different juices. For instance, just from taking a choice of one juice over another, I could tell a noticeable observable difference in the levels of sweating. I liked sauerkraut juice very much. I would drink prune juice and listen to it gurgle through and then exit in less than an hour. Sometimes I felt cravings for different tastes. I would say that there were four or five different juices that I used most often. Also, I remember drinking some clear vegetable bouillon. I drank about four to six ten-ounce glasses a day of either the juices or the bouillon. I drank a lot of water, too. This is important. A daily powerful high-stress vitamin with minerals was part of the regimen.

The big treat was carrot juice. Carrot juice took on the importance of filet mignon, chateaubriand. Carrot juice was seventh heaven! Carrot juice is a marvelous food. It's terribly rich and it's thicker than the other juices. Whenever I drank it I felt that I was cheating, as it had so much more substance than most of the other beverages, which were grapefruit juice, sauerkraut juice, bouillon, prune juice and, of course, water. I was not interested in spicy tastes, although some people might find sauerkraut juice a little spicy, and I didn't find at all that I was tempted when surrounded by food. I would sit with friends at mealtimes and not feel tempted and not feel deprived in any way. I felt fortunate at the time in the sense that I was in a supportive environment . . . a combination of a great deal of solitude and personal freedom and in my own choice of companions and activities, and the ready availability of friends and knowledgeable people.

I saw a local doctor during the fast, and he sort of looked after me. However, I didn't see him until I was forty days into the fast. In looking back, this was indeed a mistake. The changes that seem to take place, and I'm just talking about the macroscopic level of everyday personal observances, are very radical. It makes sense to check in with a doctor even before you start and, most certainly, to let the doctor track your progress.

I was interested in keeping track of what outward physiological changes I would go through during the fast. In truth, there appeared to be very few, other than an enormous weight loss. I was waiting to feel some portent that it would be a good time to end the fast, some awakening of my body. I was looking for some kind of message, a biological message telling me that I should stop fasting. However, I really didn't find any. I didn't feel ill or weak during this time. I felt elevated, exceedingly lightheaded. I could concentrate quite well. I wasn't working all the time. I thought about certain things—inventions I was working on and other types of technical processes. However, none of these activities involved any strenuous exertion. There were no time constraints, and I didn't feel my endurance was being tested in any way.

During this entire period I was basically alone and had very little interest in sex. It's not that I was avoiding it. The opportunities were not there, as I was in solitude and when you are deep into a fast your energy is out of your body and into your mind. It was a time of intense introspection. I think it's a very personal process. I was on a journey, alone, even though, in fact, I never really went anywhere except through my own body and mind. I would take walks outside and concentrate on my immediate relationship with nature and other people. I didn't plan very much. That's one thing I remember. I was very unconcerned with future plans. I had a tendency at that time to be very much involved in being able to plan things into the future, and this fast quelled that need very well. It was a means of bringing me into the present, and of allowing me to examine my own motivations, my own will, my own abilities to do certain things, my own habits.

After some forty days I decided it was time to check out with the doctor and he sent me to the hospital to take a battery of tests. I underwent the tests and there was virtually nothing out of the ordinary at all. My blood pressure was exactly 120 over 80, which I believe is textbook normal. There was something in my blood which indicated that there had been some tissue deterioration, but quite little. The doctor didn't feel that I was in any danger or that I had to end the fast immediately.

I did cut the fast short after fifty-seven days, but that was more by choice than for any necessity. I really think that my body was telling me that time that it was damn well time to stop, because I looked pretty wan, and while I don't remember any self-generated motivation to stop, I remember seizing the moment as a portent or a sign that I'm sure was internally motivated . . . so I really can't say that there was no motivation to stop.

I broke the fast by eating just spinach for four days. It was all right. Stewed spinach isn't that exciting [it's not the be all and end all], but there wasn't any problem. When I finished the fast, I had lost thirty-seven pounds. That was at the lowest point, before eating anything. I remember that just as soon as I started eating, whether because of more water or whatever, I gained back almost six pounds right away. And over the period of the next four months I gained back the weight . . . all of it! All the way back up to 215 pounds! It was very quick. I don't believe that I was really gorging myself. The problem is that part of the fasting for me was a fad diet. I would never suggest fasting to anybody on this level, because if you look at fasting as a fad diet. you avoid any basic confrontation with yourself, with your own eating habits. I don't see it as a solution to losing weight, in any permanent way at all. A diet without retaining eating habits is more than useless, but I could see fasting being used to kindle a spark in someone who needs an added impetus to lose weight.

One of the most attractive realizations of the fast is that it's a purifying process. Innately, I just felt very much purified going through this regimen. It is too simple an explanation to say that the body is throwing off all these terrible things, but I did feel that there was some self-regulation going on, some chance for the body to avoid all these things. I've read studies of hyperactive children and other cases where normal, commercially processed foods can have an immense effect on consciousness and the way you feel, both on the physical and emotional level.

I think that a long fast is not as useful as a shorter fast used regularly. There was a definite strain on my body. I had a chronic disease before going on the fast. As soon as I started eating again, it flared up, and the dictor felt that the metabolic change had triggered the reoccurrence. Luckily, it was quickly brought under control.

For myself, fasting was a self-imposed trial, a ritual, [a rite of passage.] I'm not afraid of not eating at all, and I think that this kind of knowedge itself has some inner meaning to me in my relationship in my own life. It's a strengthening attitude of being independent and able to undergo certain hardships if you are called on to do so. I know that I could fast again for that length of time and it would not be uncomfortable. Actually, it would be very pleasant and perfectly comfortable. There is a certain pleasure associated with mental changes, the exhilaration of feeling very lightheaded and physically light. The physical changes might have had something to do with it. The changes between my body image and what my body really looked like must have been important. The tensions involved in the rapid changes associated with that might have contributed to it. It was positively exhilarating at the time. I would recommend that if people want to fast, they do it under supervision and for no more than ten days to two weeks at the longest. For the same reason that fasting is not a good diet per se, because it is such a radical change, it's not easy to integrate into your daily life. Good eating habits mean that your relationship to the food that you're tempted with every day improves over what you have been brought up on. I didn't use the initial knowledge gained from my fast to change my attitude toward my compulsive eating.

On the purely physiological side, when you start fasting the frequency of bowel movement goes down. But I was having some form of bowel movement right to the end. There were still some things left in my digestive tract or intestines that was being washed or irrigated out. This shows, at least to me, that cleansing yourself is not such a simple process. You can't suddenly decide to empty yourself of negative things because this kind of bowel movement continued for a long time after I had anything solid to eat. At the beginning the bowel movements were more frequent, once a day. After about a week, they slackened down to once every few days. I did occasionally take enemas, a few times a week. Drinking prune juice had very much the same effect. I didn't really suffer from constipation as there wasn't anything from which to be constipated. If I took a large glass of prune juice, it would whiz through my body and come out through the bowels within an hour. My body had lost the ability to absorb it. Prune juice, in any event, isn't readily absorbable, and that's why it's such a good natural laxative. However, sauerkraut juice had very much the same effect for me.

I didn't exercise much. I walked a lot. I was very susceptible to chills, so I kept warm. I had a sense at the time that my resistance was not great—obviously I was under a great strain. I did coddle myself at the time. I did things I like, that interested me. I'd read, walk, very quietly, as in a retreat. I did think of it as kind of a retreat; the fact that I was completely alone was an important factor. I was able to avoid a lot of the stress that might be inherent in normal day-to-day situations. I don't think it's fair if you're going to go on a fast to subject yourself to the normal day-to-day stresses. I don't think you should fast during a week when you're working. I think that's asking too much of the body. I'm sure that fifty thousand years ago hunters weren't as active. Being weak from hunger really does mean something.

I guess the really overwhelming thing that I learned was that there is a self-regulating aspect of the body and there is something very valuable in learning your own body chemistry. It's very much like biofeedback. As a matter of fact, it was an extensive biofeedback session for me and my body. It's much the same effect as seeing the effects of different stimulants. Fasting is a stimulant, make no mistake about it. If you want to be technical about it, you could say that I was fooling around with ketones, or whatever substances in the fasting process serve to change the mental state. I was in ketosis; I was a "ketone head." The lack of food started another system of operations in my body. Thus, less food was not less bodily operation. The lack of food became the stimulant for the body to program its activities in a different mode.

The one time I was most in conflict with eating was during a wake for a friend at a fancy restaurant down in the town. The chef had prepared a number of delightful dishes as part of the tribute. There was a four-foot wok-shaped conveyance filled with lobster paella and many other things, and I remember sitting there with my little fasting grin watching all the people sitting there eating. I had strong temptations to break my fast at that point, but part of what held me back was just the fear that if I broke my fast with the wrong food, that I might kill myself, that I might actually do myself such damage, and so shock my system that I would make myself sick. I was very aware of the importance of my diet before and after the fast. My diet before the fast was meat and vegetables. I went through no preparatory change of diet. It seems to make sense to me to try a gradual change from a meat diet, because I feel that fasting was an extension of not eating meat, of having a vegetarian diet, much more so than any relationship regarding the eating of meat. Meat-eating is a very corporeal, present-oriented activity. Eating vegetables seems much more spread out in time—less concentration on the absolute moment and more of a warm continuum and less of a frantic search for an attempt to alter the environment.

I would think that it might be quite difficult to fast in the city. I once did a ten-day fast in the city, but that was all. I didn't find it difficult, but I knew that it was much much more pleasant and felt more rewarding in the country—in lovely areas. This is because you find yourself noticing the immediacy of your surroundings, noticing a much more passive feeling in your relationship to the environment. For myself it was an immense change. I don't know how this relationship was connected to the release from a meat diet, but I felt a new sense of relationship with the environment in being filled with adrenalin and energy. I was more at one with nature at this time. I felt my senses were much more acute than normal. I felt I could see and hear more accurately. I think it's a chance to concentrate on other-worldly matters and things of importance.

I remember hearing my own breathing quite a bit and also easily having the feeling of floating. Lying down felt like floating. There was a sense of suspension, even with walking—a lack of corporeality. I really think that this has a great deal to do with the early basis of religion. It makes perfect sense to send a disciple out into the desert until he has a vision. I am really into this kind of understanding through my own fasting experience. The magic isn't just the religion— it's not eating! It's the mental changes the person goes through in not eating, a partial dehydration, lack of minerals, and things of this sort. Fasting is also part of the culture of other societies, a part of a purification ritual. I think that there's something instinctive about it. Animals go off their feed when they're feeling sick. I sometimes question doctor's urging some people to eat when they're not hungry. I don't understand why the body should be fed when it's not hungry. For instance, when a person has a high fever, perhaps the body is trying to say, "Don't eat, I'm not hungry, I don't want to digest food right now." Maybe it's saying that it needs its energy for other things, marshalling its energy to fight infection, to generate new blood cells, or do whatever the body does. It's very comforting to get this kind of feeling of a sense of self-knowledge about the body's activities. It's great to have a feeling of becoming more aware of the wonderful organism you have the opportunity to inhabit and the many different central subjects involved.

Of particular interest are the cybernetic aspects involved. When I was studying physics, they told me not to anthropomorphize things, don't make inhuman things human. I remember I used to say things like "the atom 'tends' to move." But they always rebuked me, saying the atom doesn't "tend" to do anything, the atom is acted upon by outside forces. But I like to anthropomorphize things. A large part of our mythology is anthropomorphizing everything, and for God's sake, if I can't anthropomorphize my own body, that's a severe restriction on me. Thus, I tried to think of the central mechanisms of my body as being wondrously intelligent things. I don't try to classify them as tropisms or reflexes or whatever they could be called technically, but it's interesting to me to find the response of my own organism to changing invironment and how to regulate it. So there was some intellectual interest in my pursuit. Intellectually, I found that my body was a very sturdy companion—to me! A sturdy chariot. I put it through quite a lot of stress, and it took it in good spirits and showed me things about my limits of endurance I believe will stand me in good stead as I approach other endeavors.

I think the idea of fasting is to become more consciously aware of the little types of feedback, the little control loops within the body that are usually hidden from our view, the voices that your body uses to tell you thing below the level of everyday consciousness—things like "I'm hungry," "I'm thirsty," "I want minerals."

This relates to the purification aspect. If you eat processed food—and who doesn't?—you're talking about forty to fifty chemicals. You don't know what the hell is in it. How, then, do you find out how to refine your understanding of the body's needs for things? I think I have an excellent understanding of the cybernetic mechanisms involved in body functions, but their application to the way the body uses them is way beyond my knowledge. I can apply cybernetic principles on macroscopic levels, such as the control loops regulating muscles, but that sort of outlook is trendy in the sense that I would just see it as a simile for the increased sensitivity to my body's signals, which also can be achieved through the quiet isolation and environmental change involved in fasting. It can be achieved without fasting, but fasting works in this direction.

When I said that fasting works as a stimulus, I meant that there's a wild euphoria that is continuous and pervasive when you're fasting. The fast is self-stimulating—you're putting nothing into the body. The release from food stimulates other activity. The increased alertness reminded me of a mild stimulant. It was comfortable. I don't know the medical angle of ketosis, but it seemed mild. This is the way the body gets rid of its own fat. I learned that the body is a self-regulating mechanism. It gets fat because you eat more than you need right then and there. But why store it on your own person? Why not just evacuate it when you eat more? Why should there be a natural mechanism that stores it on your body? To me, that's because it's quite obvious that the body is still living in a time when food is not a certainty, and you store food because you don't know when you're going to get it later. Part of the intense alertness and the euphoria has something to do with this. The euphoria is not mind-blurring at all, none of the effects are in any way counterproductive for a hungry man stalking his prey. The reason the body creates the alertness, heightened mental state, heightened awareness to sound is because it's time to go out there and hunt. Your body is saying, "Hey look, you're really goddamn hungry, you better catch something to eat. Now I'm not going to bother you for a couple of days, I'm not going to say anything about it for a while, but to make sure you know that you have to eat soon I'm going to heighten your awareness, and you're going to be better at catching things than you were before, because you obviously couldn't hack it before. Obviously, because how did you ever *not* get to eat." That's what I mean by anthropomorphizing it. I can really see a body being like Lenny Bruce, like a Jewish mother.

In retrospect, what I see is a certain consciousness that I have in the strength of my body, and I feel that I've made peace with it. Now I have belatedly changed my eating habits. This wasn't as a direct result of the fast, but the fast contributed toward my realization that any overall change in my own relationship to food would have to be along the lines of a long-standing change. The fast is no substitute for judicious application of energy in rearranging your set of wants, and the ways that you choose to satisfy them. Nobody is going to *stay* thin by fasting. If they tried to do this on a continuous basis, there would be a deleterious effect. I've heard of people fasting one day a week. That seems to be a reasonable thing to do. It probably puts a strain on the body. It's probably not as good as a total program of eating regularly and eating healthfully.

I see a fast as a punctuation mark. Holidays punctuate our lives; New Year's punctuates the year. It's a very innate biological sense of time—such things as the way winter punctuates the year. It's good somehow to know that another year has come around and there's some difference between the seasons. I tend to think of constant environments as timeless and changeless and passive—not stimulating to get things done, to take your own life in hand, apply your energies. But even in a place which lacks seasons, people look for the small changes, the nuances that punctuate their lives.

In Oregon, when the rains let up, it's the same effect as in New York when the snow comes, and for me fasting has become the same kind of punctuation, in my continuing relationship with food and my love affair with food. Love affair? I love food, and don't let anybody tell you that fasting is not a food-oriented experience. After all, would you say that an atheist isn't involved with God?

3

WHAT HAPPENS
WHEN YOU
FAST

"It was by observing a lighter diet than the others that I was the first to perceive the danger."
> —APOLLONIUS, on the Plague of Ephesus

MOSES, JESUS, PYTHAGORAS, and Plato are among the ancient fasters who certainly must have known the strange power, the magic of the long fast. The relationship between fasting and religion or revelation is so pervasive as to leave no doubt that the fast was not a ritual derived from religion, but the actual means through which the faster met God. It was, and still is, a unique spiritual connection.

Yet how little we know about the body and how it works, about the effects of the fast on a human brain. The ancients had little medical knowledge to go on; however, they made good use of their own observations and intuitions. It is only very recently, within the past fifteen years, that medical research has turned its eyes toward fasting. Many of the hundred-odd medical studies published in this period have been stimulated by the new practice of using fasting as a therapy in

27

weight reduction for extreme cases of obesity. Doctors began to admit their patients to hospitals and have them fast for prolonged periods, a process which showed encouraging signs of success in permanent weight loss. The problem of severe complications arose: Several patients actually died during treatment, and it was obvious that a great deal of research would be necessary to determine the actual body/brain processes at work during the fast. A great deal of the published findings are tentative, many of them contradictory. But we now have the first general working picture of body metabolism during fasting.

The following pages summarize these findings. The reports have been written in the language of the medical profession. [Like it or not, these are the names of the body. We are stuck with them.] While it would be no problem to simplify and use popularized metaphors, this will not do at all. First, it detracts from the clarity of description. Second, many readers will welcome the opportunity to learn what really happens in their bodies. Third, the correct language is necessary for those readers who want to go on and read some of the medical reports for themselves. In the last instance, this chapter is an introduction to the available literature. A bibliography of medical articles will be found at the back of the book. Also, a "fasting glossary" of medical terms is included. You might want to read through it once just to get a familiarity with the terms involved.

The Metabolism of Fasting

Your fast begins two to three days after you stop eating. Technically, that is the moment when all the calories in your system are absorbed. At this point your body switches over from an external energy system to an internal circuit. In a sense, the deprivation of the normal income energy acts as a stimulus.

One way to look at it is to understand that during a fast your body listens to itself; it hears itself. It sends messages back and forth monitoring its own activities.

This is very much like electronic feedback when a machine begins to record its own operations, rather than the operations coming into it. An example is the high buzz sound you hear when you take a microphone and you bring it around to its own circuit. Basically, it is hearing itself function. This is what happens when the body switches over to a system of internal controls to maintain its own equilibrium. Your body hears the message that it is not getting anything to eat; it is not getting its fuel in the way it's used to getting it. It has to change its operations. It has to work harder.

When all your calories are absorbed, you begin a negative calorie balance. This is a moment of distinct change in your metabolism. The term *metabolism* refers to the sum of all the physical and chemical processes which either produces and maintains living substance, or breaks down matter in order to liberate heat for energy. The latter, the breaking down, is known as *catabolism*, one of the processes through which the body fuels itself during the fast.

Even when you do not eat or receive any kind of nourishment in any form, the body still needs fuel and burns a considerable number of calories. At complete rest, an average-size male will use around 1,750 calories a day. With light or moderate exercise the rate will go up to 2,000 to 2,800 calories per day, depending on weight and size. These rates are only slightly less for women.

The negative energy balance does not mean that your body has shut itself down—quite the contrary. The external, the income energy is shut off, and the body switches to its internal metabolic systems. When the income systems are off, you will notice marked decreases in the following functions of your body: respiration, circulation, peristalsis, muscle tonus, body temperature, glandular functions, and other vegetative functions of the body. These functions are measured as part of what is known as a basal metabolism rate, a measurement taken at rest after no food has been administered for fourteen to eighteen hours.

In a way, your body is going into a kind of hibernation period. Your heart slows down, you get cold very easily, bowel movement practically ceases, the blood pressure drops.

While the internal system is in operation, your body still must feed itself to supply fuel for its muscular activity and for the central nervous system. To accomplish these tasks, it mobilizes energy from various internal sources. The most obvious sources are your fat deposits. Fats are commonly stored in what are known as adipose tissues. Most of the fats of the body are called *triglycerides*. After the first few days of your fast, the triglycerides are broken down and released from the adipose tissue into the blood. This is accompanied by a marked increase in fatty acid levels in the blood. Although a lot of the broken-down fat is taken up by the peripheral tissue, much of it winds up in the liver for processing.

A very special process takes place in the liver. The excess fatty acids are converted into an intermediary substance with the long name of acetylcoenzyme A (acetyl CoA for short). This substance is a crucial component in fasting metabolism. Acetyl CoA is then broken down and serves in the synthesis of two other key substances: acetoacetic acid and beta-hydroxybutyric acid, which are collectively referred to as *ketone bodies*. The ketone-body production usually begins two or three days into the fast and serves as the major fuel for the body during the fast.

Ketosis

Once you stop eating, it takes your body two to three days to use up its stores of carbohydrates. The carbohydrates are converted into glucose, which is the prime energy substance of your body. Under normal circumstances, glucose is the only nutrient used by the brain. Carbohydrates are stored in the body as glycogen, which is a form of starch. It stays in that form until the body turns it into glucose, for use as energy.

When the carbohydrate, or glycogen, supply is exhausted, you switch over to internal ketogenic diet. This means that most of the fuel for running your body is taken from the ketone bodies which are mobilized in the liver from the fatty acids, which in turn are derived from your fat deposits. At this point, you literally begin to eat your own fat.

This point is reached very quickly as your body is able to store less than 1,000 calories of carbohydrate as glycogen, an insignificant amount that only lasts about two days after the fast begins. One theory of ketosis states that it is caused when the body is deprived of carbohydrates (and therefore of glucose), the response to which is fatty-acid oxidation. Another theory of the mechanism is that while the fats are being broken down and converted into energy sources in the liver, there is also a decrease in *lipogenesis*, the formation of fat. It has been shown that during ketosis there is both a decrease in lipogenesis, the fatty-acid synthesis, and an increase in fatty-acid oxidation, the result of the use of fat as ketone bodies to supply fuel for the body.

The ketone bodies themselves are the major energy source during fasting. They can also be expelled through the urine or exhaled through the lungs. The latter two processes are of minor importance compared to the first, which is their conversion to energy.

The ketone bodies are found in three variations: (1) acetone, (2) acetoacetic acid, and (3) betahydroxybutyric acid. Except for acetone, which arises from acetoacetic acid, they are normal products of fat metabolism. As was mentioned before, the ketone bodies are broken down in the liver from acetyl CoA and are oxidized by the muscles.

In the ketosis state, up to 70 per cent of the energy requirement usually supplied by glucose can come from the ketone bodies. The rest comes from the breakdown of lean tissues, a process called *gluconeogenesis*, in which glucose is created from molecules (protein and fat) which are not themselves carbohydrates.

Two symptoms of ketosis are a bad taste in the mouth and slight nausea. The bad taste and bad breath are not due to the elimination of so-called "toxic" substances, but are the result of the production of acetone—one of the ketone bodies—in the liver, which is then exhaled through the lungs. The taste in your mouth will not go away, but it can be helped by chewing sugarless gum or using a mouthwash. The nausea is usually slight, and contributes to the anorexia—lack of appetite—of fasting. Whenever you begin to think of food, you will get slightly nauseated. This is one of the main reasons why hunger is usually never a problem during a long fast.

The ketosis of prolonged fasting is quickly reversible through the injection of either glucose or insulin. When this happens, the production of ketone bodies in the liver abruptly stops. This process takes only about five minutes.

The Fasting High

Under ordinary circumstances, glucose is the only nutrient which can supply energy for the brain. When you fast, as we have seen, the carbohydrate stores are quickly depleted. Only a relatively small amount of glucose is available. This comes from gluconeogenesis, in which the glucose is metabolized from proteins and, to a very limited extent, from fat stores.

This situation is something of a puzzle to medical researchers. We know that we can fast for extended periods of time in relative safety, for far longer than the time it would take to use up all our carbohydrate stores and all our proteins for gluconeogenesis in order to maintain the stable and necessary supply of glucose to power the brain.

Yet, although the carbohydrate (glycogen) stores are quickly depleted, the protein, or lean muscle and tissues stores, are conserved rather well. What happens is that instead of using the unavailable carbohydrates or relying on gluconeogenesis for glucose, your brain switches over to a different fuel system altogether and uses ketone bodies to replace the glucose. Thus, the body is able to store fuel in a most economical way, by transforming materials which are not even fuels under normal circumstances. Perhaps this was a primitive adaptation from the time when man was in the wilderness and needed all the muscle tissue he could conserve during long periods without food. The point is that the fat is readily expendible for ketone-body utilization, which has proved to be a reliable nutrient for the brain. Thus the process of gluconeogenesis, which is mainly protein breakdown, is not primarily used.

The key to the euphoria, the hallucinogenic high that often accompanies a fast, is due to changes in the oxidation in the brain. Consider the example of a long-distance runner. Anyone who has jogged for a long distance or even run for just two or three miles, knows a sense of euphoria. This develops as an oxic state, a low-oxygen state. You burn up your glucose, then you start to go on glycogen and other substances. You are not burning fat, but you are in an anoxic state, one in which less oxygen is available. You have blown it off. Your breathing is hard, and as you breathe you blow off more oxygen. A similar type of euphoria exists in fasting and is related to the low-oxygen state encountered in long-distance running.

Fasting results in a low-oxygen state. The uptake of the ketone bodies is significant. They account for 60 percent of the brain's consumption of oxygen (52 percent by beta-hydroxybutyric acid, and 8 percent by acetoacetic acid) as opposed to glucose, which accounts for only 29 percent of the brain's oxygen consumption. Thus there is much less oxygen available when ketone bodies are used as fuel.

In a normal situation, only glucose can be oxidized rapidly enough by the brain to maintain its equilibrium. The uptake of oxygen by the ketone bodies is quite different than the normal situation, in which glucose is responsible for oxygen consumption. The doubling of the rate of oxidation alone perhaps explains the fasting high associated with the prolonged fast. This condition could very well be responsible for the change in consciousness to a revelatory, spiritual mode. In this sense, the spirit might have a home in the biochemistry and metabolics of the brain.

Another fascinating point is that ketone bodies are not usually found in the brain in any significant numbers during a normal state. It is only during ketosis that they are used as a glucose replacement. This is the period when the change in the oxidation leads to visions and euphoria—the fasting high. Interestingly enough, it turns out that one of the ketone-body substrates, beta-hydroxybutyric acid, although negligible in the adult brain, is an active force in young, developing brains. As the brain matures, the use of this substance gradually comes to a halt. But it can be noted that this particular ketone body uses up twice as much oxygen as glucose, and this mechanism can perhaps give us some insight into the wonders, the awe which we all experience in childhood, a sensitivity that we somehow seem to lose when we grow into adults.

There is another way to look at the fasting high, a step away from the medical, metabolic model into the systems approach of cybernetics. Going back to the idea of feedback, in ketosis, you get distortion. Your body is not hearing what it is used to. The loop is broken. Suddenly you feel that things are longer or higher or straighter or thicker, whatever, and this has nothing to do with the external stimulus. What is happening is that you are not processing the internal stimulus with the same degree of expertise that your senses are used to getting. Your body and brain are working under a new set of conditions, basically internally generated. The external stimulus either is shut off or comes in a new way, a way in which the body is unfamiliar.

In your normal state, there is income-energy activity. You are constantly taking stuff in, breaking it down, as the molecules go from a more complex to a less complex state. The loss of complexity has to do with the oxidation process, the process which allows the blood to carry oxygen throughout the system. The oxygen is used to provide a way of metabolizing or producing energy transforms in the cells. That is normal. In the abnormal ketosis, the molecular configurations which basically come from fatty acids are used in place of the income energy fuel, and so instead of breaking down something which the body gets from the outside, it begins to break down things that exist inside itself.

This creates an emergency situation for your body. Everything goes to helping your brain. Your body slows down, and there is a shift from the parasympathetic and orthosympathetic systems (the autonomic systems) to cerebral functioning. This accounts for distortion in the feedback systems, and along with the production of the previously mentioned oxygen-carrying ketone bodies, helps to give us a picture of why you get high and euphoric when you fast.

Protein Breakdown

Along with fat metabolism, the protein stores of the body are also broken down, but to a much smaller extent. When the glycogen supplies of your body are exhausted, the brain will use ketone bodies as its primary source of energy. However, it still has an appetite for carboyhydrates. This appetite is appeased through protein catabolism, the breaking down of amino acids (protein) through gluconeogenesis. This process, which takes place in the liver, is crucial to the ability of your body to withstand a long fast. During the fast period your body has to burn both fat and protein stores as sources of energy. But your body cannot live on fat sources alone, as the normal carbohydrate levels in the blood require a certain amount of protein breakdown. There is, however, a mechanism to conserve these nitrogenous protein stores. Much of the breakdown occurs during the first few days of the fast. There is a certain loss of muscle mass. This is unavoidable. After a while, however, this breakdown is reduced. There appears to be a conservation mechanism that starts to work on about the tenth day of the fast. At that point there is usually a measurable decline in the previously great losses of nitrogen, urea nitrogen, and uric acid, all measures which point to a breakdown of body protein.

One explanation of this safety-valve activity is that on about the tenth day, your body goes through hormonal changes. Thyroid function is decreased, and there is increased secretion of growth hormone. These two activities result in decreased protein breakdown and increased mobilization of fat deposits.

One thing you have to realize about fasting: The weight you lose during the fast is made up of both fats and muscle tissue. There is a certain breakdown of lean tissue, and this is not a very good thing for the body. During the first thirty days of a fast, the average-size male will lose about two and a half pounds of protein, which means that eleven pounds of lean tissue has been broken down. This drops down considerably in the next thirty days when the lean-tissue loss is only around six pounds. The loss of protein and lean tissue are reflected in the nitrogen excretion through the urine, which should be measured before and during the fast. The level will depend quite a bit on your prefast diet.

Carbohydrates and "Hunger Diabetes"

The total deprivation of carbohydrates during fasting forces the body to totally alter its normal carbohydrate metabolism. The new condition is a diabetes-like state characterized by ketosis and less use of glucose. The state is often called "hunger diabetes" or "fasting hypoglycemia." The mechanism for this condition is not yet clearly defined. It is known, however, that while your body is in this condition there is an intolerance to glucose and a lessening of insulin secretion. One theory is that there is an impairment of the liver function which is responsible for removing glucose (the hepatic glucose-removal system). This affects the production of carbohydrates from the amino acids (protein) and fatty acids. It is felt that the slowdown in this gluconeogenesis function is the focus point for the carbohydrate metabolism during fasting. Evidently there is an elevation of the enzymes which promote this metabolic process, and a suppression of those enzymes which promote glucose utilization.

Glucose intolerance means that your body is not able to use its glucose. It can be attributed to the stress situation in which your body is placed or perhaps to the depletion of potassium, a noted by-product of fasting. The carbohydrate intolerance does not increase as the fast goes on. Also, it is usually fairly mild, and much less severe than that encountered in diabetes. It totally reverses itself when the fast is broken and refeeding begins.

Fat Loss

It has proved very difficult to get an accurate measure of the exact amount of fat lost as part of the total body composition during fasting. However, two separate testing techniques came up with the same figure. Fat loss constitutes 34 per cent of the total body weight lost during a prolonged fast.

This figure seems in line with a common-sense approach to examining fat loss. Consider that 3,500 calories can be considered the equivalent of one pound of fat. During fasting, about 2,500 calories a day are burned up. Thus, it would take you a day and a half to lose one pound of fat tissue. During this same period, the total weight loss would be about three pounds. Thus, it can be seen that the adipose fat tissue accounts for about one third of the total weight loss.

During the fast only about 100 to 150 calories consumed per day come from the protein supply, which compared with the fat stores, are much more efficiently stored in the body. As the fast proceeds, the adipose fat tissues are used in increasing proportions as a source of energy, while the potassium-rich stores are spared.

Weight Loss

The amount of weight you will lose on a total fast depends on several factors: the length of the fast, the prefast diet, your own weight, amount of fat, size, and metabolism. As a rule of thumb, with total caloric deprivation with unlimited amounts of water or non-caloric beverage, you can expect to lose up to three pounds during the first twenty-four hours. During the next ten days, the average loss will be about two pounds per day. In one study of normal healthy males of average weight, the loss for the first ten days of fasting averaged sixteen pounds each. This weight loss was equal to almost 10 percent of total body weight of the people on the fast.

After the first ten days the rate of loss gradually declines from almost two pounds a day to about three quarters of a pound per day by the sixtieth day. In some cases, the loss will be totally progressive and predictable, and in others it can be irregular and unpredictable. The pattern depends on your kidney function and how much urine you excrete.

The composition of the weight loss is still not exactly determined. Fat accounts for roughly one third of the weight loss, body water accounts for one half, and the remainder is made up of protein, carbohydrates, and skeletal tissue. Carbohydrates, stored in the body as glycogen, are used up in about two days and are insignificant in terms of weight loss. Also, the skeleton is stable and contributes little in this respect.

"Starvation Acidosis"

Ketone bodies are highly acidic in nature. When there is an overproduction, as in ketosis, the acid balance builds up to an abnormal level, creating a condition called *acidosis*. The condition is diagnosed through notation of excessive ketone bodies in the highly acidic urine and indicates a high degree of alkalinity in the blood and body tissues. This variety of acidosis is known as "starvation acidosis."

Starvation acidosis causes dangerous imbalances in the bodily systems designed to conserve water and electrolytes (sodium, potassium). The acidosis begins a few days after the onset of ketosis and is responsible for very large amounts of body water lost during the first week to ten days of the fast. The onset of acidosis, the subsequent body-water loss, is an indication of a strain on the renal (kidney) system of the body. This can be very dangerous if there is any congenital or reoccurring kidney malfunction.

Water and the Electrolytes

About one half of the body-weight loss during fasting is due to body-water loss. The mechanisms for this loss are not yet completely defined. In fact, they are much more complex than would seem natural, as the initial rapid weight loss in fasting, mostly water, is a great deal more than would be expected in terms of caloric expenditure.

The highly negative water balances result in body hypohydration, which is a state of decreased water content in the blood. Also, there are large mineral losses which go hand in hand with the large water loss. These mineral losses mainly consist of sodium and potassium.

Sodium: Sodium losses are part of a double-edged pattern in fasting. First, there is a quick loss due to sodium withdrawal—lack of salt intake—and second, at the same time there is the development of acidosis, which causes the peak of urinary sodium excretion after four or five days of fasting.

Most of the major dangers of fasting are related to sodium depletion and concomitant losses of body water and related kidney function impairment. Thus, the conservation of salt is an important aspect to the success and good health of a fast. The depletion of sodium to any great extent can lead to grave complications and must not be allowed to develop.

There is no clear picture as yet to why fasting results

in sodium loss. Such a loss can be as much as two grams per day.

Potassium: Potassium loss during fasting can average as much as 1.5 grams per day. This amount is enough to create a severe deficiency, which can result in a breakdown in renal homeostasis.

What normally happens is that a significant amount of urinary potassium is passed through the urine during the first ten days of the fast. This indicates two things: first, a poor kidney response to the potassium withdrawal, and second, the continued absorption of potassium through residue foods remaining in the intestinal tract.

This pattern slows down considerably when the kidney adjusts and the body begins to increase its mobilization of fat deposits and, at the same time, begins to spare the potassium-rich protein.

During fasting, you must take a significant amount of potassium as a supplement, or after thirty days you will notice a significant development of weakness, lethargy, lassitude, and nausea. Such supplements are available in pill form. Another symptom of potassium depletion may also be postural hypotension (very low blood pressure), which is common during prolonged fasting and could be caused in part by decreased potassium content of smooth muscle fibers in the blood vessel walls.

Anorexia

One of the most significant and amazing aspects of fasting is the total lack of appetite after the first few days. This lack of appetite is called *anorexia*. This syndrome explains why people over the centuries have been able to maintain themselves over long periods of time with no foods. They are simply not hungry! As a matter of fact, the normal appetite virtually vanishes during the long fast, while on a low-calorie diet, the hunger is usually intolerable. This is one reason fasting is now used for weight-losing therapy, whereas low-calorie diets usually end in terrible hunger and failure.

One common effect of anorexia is that you really do not have any need or desire to eat again, and hunger is rarely, if ever, the reason a fast is broken. In most cases, people on supervised fasts will want to continue. The anorexia associated with short- and long-term fasts is not to be confused with *anorexia nervosa*, an illness that afflicts mostly teenage girls. The syndrome reflects a physiological inability to eat over an extended period of time. It is usually successfully treated as a psychological disorder.

Refeeding Edema

After the fast is broken, you will stand to gain a large, seemingly unwarranted amount of weight. This gain is far out of proportion to the amount of calories consumed during the initial refeeding. It is known as *refeeding edema,* a condition in which the body tissues contain an excessive amount of tissue fluid. There is an expansion of the intracellular and extracellular fluid space. One explanation is that the edema is controlled by high levels of aldesterone, a hormone produced in the adrenal cortex of the brain, which is important to the regulation of the metabolism of sodium, chloride, and postassium. Another theory states that it is proportional to sodium intake. In any event, there is usually a spontaneous remission after fifteen to twenty days, but only after you have gained back a considerable amount of the body weight lost during the fast.

Diuretics are frequently used to alleviate this condition. Also helpful are quantities of potassium chloride and sodium chloride in mineral supplements used in conjunction with the fast.

The key thing to keep in mind is that by entering into a fast, you are asking your body to switch over to an internal system of equilibrium. The external income energy (calories) is cut off, and your body must make do on its own resources. The changes are swift and radical. After just two or three days you will begin to feel very different, and for very good reason: The lack of food acts as a stimulus to alter your internal body chemistry.

The question of monitoring is very important. Under orinary eating circumstances, you have a built-in set of checks and balances learned since infancy. You know what you are putting into your body and how it will affect you, for better or worse. During a fast, you are in foreign territory. The normal signposts and warning signals will not help you. As we have seen, the fasting metabolism is far from simple. Indeed, when there is no caloric intake, your body loses not only fat, but also protein stores, fluids, and salts, and these latter three elements account for well over half the weight loss. The only way to check the danger point of such losses is through careful monitoring, and you cannot monitor yourself. Your friends cannot do it for you either. The changes that occur in the blood and urine are not visible to the naked eye. Careful medical supervision during an extended fast is a necessity.

4

STORY OF A CLEAN-OUT FAST

"The pagans give New Year's gifts; you, give alms! They find amusement in licentious songs; you entertain yourselves with the instruction of Holy Scripture! They run to the theatre, you to the church; they drink to excess, you keep a fast! If you are not able to keep a fast today, at least partake of food with moderation."

—St. Augustine

DAVID AND JO-ANN *live in an old renovated church in up-state New York. Jo-Ann is a yoga instructor and is a sculptor. They recently spent four years in India and Japan on Fulbright scholarships. While in India, they lived in an ashram and studied with a yogi who is also an M.D.:*

We started in India, where we lived at our ashram. Our teacher told us that we had to go on a very big, deep clean-out and fast, and we did it according to our astrological tantric signs. In other words, everybody has a number according to when they were born. David is a two, I'm a nine, and you have to fast according to your number. I have to fast nine days. Anything less than nine days is not a real fast. David has to go in multiples of two. The least he can fast is for eleven days—that is, if he wants to be in cycle with his sign, with his number.

You start on your cycle day of one. There's a system in which you work out the day you start the fast, and on that day it takes very little energy to start. It's a very simple, easy matter to go your whole duration. According to your chart, you go up to three days. Between days three and four there is a drop and you have to be very careful—your whole energy drops. This chart was really a chart of our energy up to nine days. It's a nine-day cycle.

We have found, in our experience, that the end of the third day is the hardest part of the fast, but of course for some people the first day is the hardest part. On the third day the energy starts to drop because the body is recycling itself. That's the whole thing about the fast, you're resynching. It's called *kyra;* it's a part of yoga. The full clean-out is eleven days. You drink a *lot* of water, and you must take enemas every three days. Enemas are very important, because your body is still making waste materials, and if you don't take enemas your body becomes toxic. The enemas ars necessary to get rid of the wastes the body is making. You have to constantly get rid of these wastes because the body continually produces energy, creating cells, and these cells are in turn creating waste materials. So, after three days, on the morning of the fourth day, you must take an enema and repeat every three days.

We do the whole clean-out fast four times a year, quarterly, seasonally. You have to do it according to seasons because you have to change your blood. We find it a terrific energizer. You're terrifically high and energetic. Physical work can be a little trying, but not as trying as people would think. People tend to think that you get weak, lie around, but that never happens to us. Sometimes when I overwork my heart will speed a little, and maybe I won't have quite as much energy. But you're not weak for initial tasks. What happens is that you become very centered when fasting, so you know how to use the energy better and you don't waste anything. It's comparable to turning on. When you turn on, you become very centered in relation to objects and things. That kind of zeroing in—there are lots of drugs that will do it—is what fasting does. After four or five days, you get very high and that high helps you to zero in on things. You're very vulnerable, too. Your psyche is very open and emotionally you're shaky. As a general rule, you should do it with some kind of supervision after three days. In our case, our teacher was an M.D. There was one man who developed a case of piles and needed this kind of supervisory attention.

One of the important elements of coming onto the fast is setting off the fast—probably as important as the fast itself. If you prepare your body to go on a fast, then you'll have no trouble. Start the preparations about three days prior to the fast. Slowly diminish your food intake. Go from cooked, heavy foods to light salads and on the second day go to raw foods. On the day before the fast go on liquid soups. All this slowly, and gently quiets the body. Then you begin the fast.

After the fast, use cooked foods. Plain, cooked food is best, because that's the easiest for the body to digest. When we went on a prolonged fast, we started eating raw food after the fast and we got a terrible case of dysentery. We said, "What happened? We just had a fast, our bodies are not healthy, and now we're sick!" Then someone at the ashram told us you must always eat cooked foods first because they're quieter. It should be fewer foods, more often.

We instinctively knew what to eat. First a little rice, which doesn't challenge the body, then foods such as light cheese, vegetable broth, etc.

We always looked forward to it. It's a very high time. We liken it to drugs a little, because you get some of those highs that people experience. We're going to do it now for two or three weeks. It's a matter of psyche.

It's just not a matter of the body. Whenever we feel that we want to lose a little weight, we do the fast in order to get into a new psyche. So it's not just to be thought of as a physical matter, but that changing the body with some consciousness will sugggest to people that it can change the consciousness, and then very often the consciousness does change. It's a lot of what yoga is about. When you change the body, you change the mind, and you do feel lighter and cleansed.

On the clean-out fast you lose about a pound a day. But I think you can lose weight much faster if you eat foods. By eating certain foods your body breaks down fat rather than not eating at all. Certain foods, high in protein and fat content and without carbohydrates and sugars, will metabolize fat, and what happens during the fast is that you are working on the stored fats and carbohydrates. You have to go through all of the things in your body that you use naturally, that you use up every day, and all those calories before you start working on the fat. Then when you start breaking down fat, not only are you breaking down fat, you are also breaking down protein—the lean muscle tissues.

Drinking water is very good psychologically. You have a natural instinct to want the mouth to move; you are used to it. When you drink water, you are giving the body certain kind of work to do. At the beginning of the fast, if I'm hungry I just drink a little water and it passes through me, giving the body the feeling that it's being filled.

In India, a lot of people fast one day a week. They don't really do a true fast, but such derivation as fruit fasts. They change their diet and they call it a fast, but the idea is the same. It's religious but also psychological that it's good to give the body some kind of a rest, so if they just eat curds and fruit they're giving the body some kind of rest compared with eating heavier foods. We have the feeling that in India as well as other places, a lot of the religious practices have a basis in physiology and psychology.

Sometimes we do shorter fasts. We like rice diets,

three times a day, juice fasts, fruit fasts, hot tea fasts. The one-day fast is great. Most people think you can't live a day without food. They think they must eat food. If you do it a few times and it becomes natural, your whole attitude toward food changes. That's the biggest value of fasting, along with all the health benefits—it's the change in the psyche. We have friends who go crazy if they don't have a meal. We're much too attached to food and ideas of appetite and hunger. These have to be altered. That's the most interesting aspect. It has to do with materialism. You can live so beautifully without certain things. Once you realize that you can go a day or two without food, and once this gets built into your system, then you feel very light, relaxed, and you don't have to spend time eating, or even thinking about it. It's very radical, and very simple. It's not like saying, "Let's change the government." Just a little personal thing, a day in your life.

We're very flexible about fasting. We don't fast one day a week. A lot depends on the mood. Sometimes if we have friends over and have a very rich dinner, all of a sudden the body feels that it just doesn't want to eat the next day. Fasting is such a lovely tool for people to use, and it's such power. And then you're never afraid to travel for fear of not being able to get decent, fresh nonprocessed foods. You don't have to go looking around for a restaurant, especially if you're a vegetarian. You know that you can get by very nicely without eating anything at all. The biggest problem we have in this area is being emotionally tied to food. The whole emotional base that food is for many people is incredible. It's a comfort, a substitution. And the amazing thing is that the emotional base is invisible. We really can't see it. For instance, the reason so many poor people in our society are fat is because they can't emotionally deprive themselves of food. It's the one thing they hold on to. The one thing that fasting can do for you is to render visible this invisible dependence on food and show you how to break the emotional dependency.

What fasting can also do is lead to a lighter diet. When a person realizes that he or she can eat nothing, perhaps the next stop is to eat lighter, to realize that it's not necessary to eat all the heavy foods.

It depends on where you want your energy. If you want to be really down to earth and based in reality, then you eat meat and heavy foods and the kind of things that keep you down on the ground. If you want to be spacy, free, and light, you'll eat the kinds of things that keep you that way, which is very little. Most speedy people hardly eat.

When we lived in Japan, it was amazing because we changed our diet completely. We had been meat-eating in America. There, we began eating fish. Our diet changed, and so did the quantity, since the Japanese people we knew ate tiny portions. We couldn't imagine how they could live. After a year and a half, we came back to America and we realized just how much food Americans eat—and what they eat! The quantity is quite amazing. People feel that they have to have different tastes, so they have multicourse meals. They're always whetting their appetites. Eating is like appetite stimulation, sensory stimulation, rather than a response to the fact that your body really needs food for activity and energy. Actually, food shouldn't be too bland, because to keep a variety in food it is necessary to have different and distinctive tastes. Otherwise, desire would fall away completely, and we wouldn't eat. It's been our experience that after we go on our fast we feel like we don't want to eat. The mind says you don't have to eat again—you feel so free.

5

THE FAT
FAST

"Every request needs humility of spirit. Fast then, and you will receive from the Lord what you ask."
—HERMES, "The Shepherd" A.D. 150

IF YOU ARE very overweight, if you have tried everything—low-calorie diet, no-carbohydrate diet, water diets, amphetamines and other drug aids—and nothing works, then perhaps fasting offers some hope.

Since 1959, doctors have been conducting "fat fasts" under medical supervision at hospitals, clinics, or rehabilitation centers. The patient checks in and undergoes a total fast for up to (or even more than) two months. The results have been coming in, and there is strong evidence that this last-resort method works for enough people to make it a viable alternative to the more conventional methods. One study shows that up to 40 percent of chronically overweight people can, and do, maintain the weight they lose during prolonged fasting. And these are people who have tried and failed with everything else. Although .40 isn't a great batting average, it does hold out hope to four out of every ten individuals who heretofore were doomed to live in a prison of fat for the rest of their lives.

There is not, and never has been, any doubt that you will lose weight, and a lot of it, very quickly during a total fast. What has happened is that the fasting research of the last fifteen years has led to new methods of studying the subject of the body and fasting and has shed new light on how these processes work.

Here are the beneficial aspects of a fat fast:

(1) You lose weight very rapidly—up to two pounds a day.

(2) Unlike the low-calorie diet, there is no hunger at all after a few days.

(3) There is a mental euphoria associated with fasting, well-documented through the ages, now located firmly in physiological processes.

(4) At the end of a long fast you will feel like eating much less than when you began.

(5) There is a very real sense of feedback. You see yourself changing very rapidly, you gain a sense of will, of self-control, a sense of being able to handle your weight problem.

(6) You will probably feel wonderful emotionally in a new "thin" body.

Two arguments against fasting for weight reduction stand out. First, although there is always a large weight loss, the chances are more than 50 percent that you will regain it all over time. The remarkable losses are not necessarily permanent and as such, the fat fast has to be considered as part of a larger program in which the fast is just one of the components. Second, there are dangers. Fasting on a prolonged scale has been compared to major surgery, or potent drugs. Make no mistake about it—it's not for everyone. Check with your doctor and find out if you are the sort of psychological and physical specimen that can withstand such a radical regimen.

Results

There is equivocal evidence on the effectiveness of fat fasts. The results seem to point to the fact that short-term fasts are ineffective while long-term fasts hold out genuine hope. In 1968, one study of twenty-five people who fasted for two weeks showed that twenty-three regained all their weight after the fast, while two maintained a loss of twenty-eight pounds. However, one of these individuals developed psychiatric problems and lost his job. Other studies have shown that there is little difference between the success rates of short-term fasts or conventional slimming methods for the chronically fat. However, it's not impossible to keep the weight off: Another study of a short fast showed that eleven out of forty-six people who fasted for two weeks lost more weight during a followup period of a year and a half. Since short-term fasting has been generally ineffective for losing weight, doctors usually only employ it when an immediate drastic reduction in weight is necessary.

The prognosis for the prolonged (one month to two months) fast is much more encouraging. Many of the benefits of fat fasts render themselves visible only after about a month. The strong motivation, the feedback on a visual level, the sense of control, are not easily established. It's not an overnight process. Those individuals who fast their way all the way down to their ideal weight have a much greater chance of staying that way.

Who Should Try a Fat Fast

You could be a candidate for a fat fast if (1) you are at least 40 percent over your ideal weight, (2) you have tried all the conventional reducing methods, and (3) the weight you lose through conventional methods is put back on. In addition you must be able to assume the financial cost of a long medically supervised process and also to deal with the social burden of leaving work and/or family for an extended period of time, thus disrupting not only your life but also the lives of those around you.

You should be between the ages of sixteen and fifty-five and be free of the following problems: gout, diabetes mellitus, liver problems, poor kidney function, serious heart disease, psychiatric illness. The critical factor is your own head. Some doctors employ psychological motivation tests to protect people from their own best intentions. Some people want to fast and think they can do it, but when the task is at hand, food addiction is so strong that nothing, not even a prolonged fast, will help.

How a Fat Fast Is Conducted

The first step is admission to either a hospital or clinic. The smaller, more intimate, and less hospital-like the environment, the better off you will be. A sanatorium atmosphere offers more diversions, a more relaxing environment than the metabolic ward of a large hospital. During the fast you will need daily medical supervision, but you are not "ill," and large-hospital services are not necessary.

One month appears to be the minimum length of time to "break" the compulsive eater. One of the reasons that short-term fasting has failed is that there has not been enough time for the patient to break off the intimate emotional relationship with food. It takes at least a month of total restriction to have the time to reflect on going without food, the changes that it makes, and just the fact that it is possible. During this period no food is given whatsoever, since even the smallest morsel will detract from the new psychological head-set of the reformed food addict.

Liquids are supplied and you are urged to drink them. You will need a lot of liquid during the fast, but the anorexia associated with the fast, the lack of appetite, tends to limit even this kind of consumption. During the first week you get only water. Starting with week two, diet sodas and fruit juices are provided, as are coffee or tea with very little added milk.

The liquid diet is supplemented by daily high-stress vitamin-mineral pills. In addition, potassium supplements are given several times daily. These supplements not only guard your present health but help to minimize the problems associated with refeeding at the end of the fast.

The staff gives you a daily checkup. Blood pressure is checked against the possibility of postural hypotension. Urine is analyzed for the ketone-body content. On a weekly basis, tests are made of uric acid, blood urea, plasma electrolytes, and pH of bicarbonate. Your liver functions will be carefully monitored, and electrocardiograms are given regularly.

After a few days, an unpleasant taste develops in your mouth, with associated bad breath. This is a usual side effect of ketosis. You will be allowed to use mouthwash or perhaps chew sugarless gum to deal with the problem.

At the beginning of the fast, some doctors prescribe a laxative to clean out the intestines. During the fast the mechanical functions of the bowel close down, and there is a possibility that preexisting food will become impacted.

Exercise is encouraged, but only in strict moderation. There is a diminution of energy during the prolonged fast; you are weaker and cannot overdo strenuous activity. The most advisable form of exercise is walking. Hot baths and showers are avoided, as they can lead to fainting.

There are frequent consultations with either your doctor or the staff psychiatrist or psychologist. The mental environment is crucial for the conduct of a successful fast. Because of this, visits home are not encouraged for the first month.

At the conclusion of the fast, you will probably stay on a few days for the initial refeeding period. Termination of a prolonged fast and the refeeding usually results in what seems to the patient to be an unwarranted gain in weight. This is refeeding edema, in which the body fills up with fluids. The psychological stress of seeing pounds and pounds go right back on even though you are on a severely restricted caloric diet, can be very trying. You will gain weight back after the fast, but it can be minimized or taken off again. It's a good idea to work out this period under medical supervision where appropriate medications can be prescribed and the transition period eased.

Part of the total program involved educational sessions on the nature of food and diet. When you leave the hosiptal in your thin body, you don't want to go out into the world with your fat mind. One kind of training deals with a program of one-to-two-day outpatient fasts every week.

Most doctors do not advise prolonged fasting in excess of a two-month period. At this point, the weight loss decreases and the vital signs begin to noticeably slow down. The euphoria fades and weakness sets in.

At this point, a restricted low-calorie diet is indicated. The refeeding, the breaking of the fast, usually begins with tea with sugar which is given for two or three days before solid food. During this time the ketosis will be reversed, and the body will be prepared to resume an intake of solid food. A small amount of food, usually from 300 to 500 calories per day, depending on your size, will be permitted. One doctor recommends the following 300-calorie-per-day diet:

Breakfast
2 eggs prepared without fat
coffee or tea without cream or sugar

Lunch
1½ oz. lean meat
½ cup cooked vegetable or salad with vinegar and
    lemon juice
black coffee or tea without cream or sugar

Dinner
1½ oz. meat or 1 heaping tablespoon of cottage
    cheese

½ cup cooked vegetable or salad with vinegar or
    lemon juice
black coffee or tea without cream or sugar

The buildup in caloric intake must be slow and
gradual. First, your body cannot tolerate a large
amount of food. Second, your body has adjusted to a
much lower metabolism rate. This lower metabolic
functioning means that you are burning much fewer
calories. A sudden jump to a normal diet will mean
that your body is confronted with what, at that time, it
will treat as an abnormal amount of food. Thus, you
can gain back a lot of unnecessary weight. It normally
takes about two to three weeks for the metabolism to
get back to normal. During that time, the refeeding
edema will subside.

The Psychological Effects of Fat Fasts

The abnormally fat person can stand a long fast,
usually both physiologically and mentally. The average
person would be courting disaster by fasting for two
months, but the fat individual has a wealth of food
within the fat stores. On the psychological side of
things, the dramatic change in the drastic weight loss is
usually enough to compensate for the considerable
stress of the long fast.

Other than general malaise, irritability, and some de-
pression, there does not seem to be a great psychological risk in prolonged fasting. Various studies have
shown that you can perform normal mental functions,
perform basic mental tasks, and so on. Problems may
arise in the following areas.

(1) There is a preoccupation with food, the idea of
    food, past relationships with food.
(2) Problems arise from visits home. Families often
    try to undermine the progress of the fast by
    urging the patient to "eat a little" when they are
    at home.
(3) All kinds of psychosexual dilemmas can arise

when a spouse is suddenly confronted with a "thin" partner, thereby unbalancing a particular sex scene.

(4) Many patients revert to immature, even infantile behavior, demanding and getting inordinate amounts of attention from doctors and nurses, competing with the other patients in various respects.

(5) The doctor can be placed in the role of all-knowing guru. Overvaluation of the relationship by the patient can be a difficulty.

(6) The successful fast will result in dramatic weight loss not necessarily accompanied by the psychological transition. This is probably the greatest problem. An individual who has been grossly fat all his life will not have had the time to readjust his private body-image in the short time of the weight loss. Thus, the patient will walk out of the clinic in a thin body but be totally unprepared for a "thin life." In their head they will still "know" they are fat. Working on this problem takes a lot of time and patience.

In general, the prolonged fast is not as stressful as might be imagined. Within the clinic or hospital there will inevitably be people under a similar program, and this lends the support of a similarly motivated group. So many drastic things are happening that success appears evident, and thus motivation is not a problem. Serious problems seldom arise. Beyond all this is the probability that patients will actually enjoy the fast. People really do like it once they are into it. They will not be hungry, and an amazing transformation will take place before their eyes.

The "Thin Future"

Once the fast is successfully completed, there is the need to face a "thin future." This means new clothes, it means sex, it means a total reorientation to many aspects of your life. Some grossly overweight people have a nonexistent sex life. Suddenly they are thin and beautiful, and meet someone new who doesn't know their personal history. It could turn into a heavy emotional trip. Imagine, some people have never been able to sit in a normal chair in a restaurant, have never gone to a movie house because they could not fit in the seat. For people like this, the thin future can be very traumatic. A balance has to be struck between the new body and the old mind. This is the key area for post-fast psychological counseling which involves not only the patient, but husbands, wives, and families.

The Dangers of Prolonged Fasting for Weight Reduction

Do not let anyone tell you different: Prolonged fasting is a serious business. It is important to have proper and adequate supervision, even after the first few days. Since 1959 there have been twelve deaths reported in medical journals which have been directly related to fasting. The severity of the dangers in this respect are magnified because (1) all these deaths took place in situations where the patient was under the care of a doctor in a hospital-like situation, and (2) these are documented instances within the medical profession; there is no way of knowing how many people have either died or suffered adversely from prolonged fasts undertaken without medical supervision.

The causes of the reported deaths included lactic acidosis, renal failure (kidney dysfunction), heart problems, acute vovulvus of the small bowel, and difficulties related to refeeding after a successful fast.

Short of death, a number of serious side effects can and do arise. Many of these are reasons for suspending the fast immediately. This is why your doctor will carefully monitor your various physical processes. The following problems have been encountered:

—postural hypotension (there is almost always a fall in blood pressure)

—fluctuations in urinary excretion of sodium and potassium, which reflects a problem in kidney function
—arterial arrhythmias (constriction of the arteries)
—menstrual irregularities
—vitamin deficiences
—alteration (obliteration) of the male sex drive
—considerable initial loss of muscle mass
—psychological stress
—general malaise
—abdominal pain
—slight nausea
—glucose intolerance
—growth of hair and nails slowed
—hair loss in women
—unpredictable metabolic and biochemical changes

The Prognosis for Fat Fasts

In the light of all these possible complications, why fast? The current thinking is that the dangers of gross obesity are reason enough to render the attendant risks of the prolonged fast acceptable. Thousands of people have been successfully treated and have been helped to new levels of health they never dreamed of before. The prolonged fast is a severe form of therapy, but in some cases it is clearly warranted.

The dangers involved usually deal with fluctuations in body fluid and the ability to conserve the protein stores of the body through a long period of caloric deprivation. The decision must be taken in regard to the individual's personal health.

6

HOW TO BE
A HUNGER
ARTIST

*"What shall I say about the fast of this faster?
I am not able to draw a picture because its beauty
overwhelms me."*

—JAMES OF SARUGH

*"Anoint your lips with the fats of a black ass, a
spotted goat, and a black bull, and rub your body
with styrax oil."*

—The Great Magic Papyrus of Paris,
on preparing for a fast

Fasting: Fact and Fancy

ALMOST ALL THE available books on the subject of
fasting were written prior to the development of modern medical fasting research. For instance, the best
book I have found is Arnold Ehret's *Rational Fasting,*
written in 1912. This book is still reprinted and re-
issued even though it was written not only before I was
born, but before my parents were born!

Thus, most people who are interested in fasting have
to rely on interpretations of medical knowledge at least

59

fifty years old, and there is no way of knowing if those interpretations are responsible judgments or mere quackery. What is clear is that Ehret's book, and the many others based on similar information, have been rendered inaccurate just by the passing years. What may have been valuable insight in terms of personal observations about the workings of the body, now becomes irresponsible conjecture in the light of highly developed medical testing techniques. What has changed is not only objective knowledge of our bodies, but ways of seeing and knowing ourselves. Many of the changes your body goes through during a fast are invisible to observation by yourself or others. Your body will not necessarily tell you or send you signals when to stop a fast. Yet the invisible processes of the body are very visible through medical tests developed during recent years, which can and should be administered during a fast. The fasting pioneers of the early part of this century did not have the benefit of these developments. Working, so to speak, in the dark, they certainly did a creditable job, but in light of today's knowledge, their views leave much to be desired.

There are three claims generally made for fasting, in the older books, which seem to be more self-serving for the proponents than accurate:

First, fasting has been presented as a cure-all for any and all diseases. Some fasting books give three quarters of their pages over to miracle cures for everything from weak fingernails to terminal cancer. Don't believe them.

Second, the idea is proposed that fasting somehow helps to eliminate "sick tissue." This goes under the name of the "autolysis" theory. Much of the fasting literature is taken verbatim from ancient Greek medical knowledge. The term *autolysis* is taken from the Greek phrase which means "self-loosing." The idea behind this theory is that sick tissue is disintegrated by enzymes generated in the cells. Autolysis is presented as a process of self-digestion and absorption. One so-called expert calls it "burning rubbish."

The problem with this theory is that while the body does break down tissue during a fast, it has no way of differentiating between "sick" and "well" tissue. True, fat deposits are burned to a greater degree than lean tissue, but there is nothing wrong per se with fat tissue, especially if you are not overweight, and the fact remains that during a fast, a significant amount of lean tissue is destroyed. If you overdo it and fast too long, you can cause permanent brain damage. Some cases have revealed deaths caused by breakdown of organ tissue, such as the heart, due to fasts which have gone too long.

The body is composed of a myriad of complex metabolic processes. There are conversions, chemical reactions, etc. The old ideas of "cause and effect" are too simplistic to explain our physiology with any degree of accuracy. The "autolysis theory" has one thing going for it: It sounds good. Someone tells you that you can clean out the sick tissue and burn the rubbish of your body. Well, it does sound enticing. So you go on a fast and positively believe that what the theory promises is happening. In fact, there is no basis for this theory in scientific evidence.

Third, a similar theory is that of "internal toxema." We supposedly accumulate "toxins" (a Greek word for poisons) in our bodies through the foods we eat. The "cleansing" properties of the organs are activated by the fast to eliminate this internal toxemia. Once again, it sounds great. Who wouldn't like to eliminate the poisons, the "internal toxemia" of their bodies? But it just doesn't wash in the light of modern theories.

In a way, all three of these theories seem to be based on a religious motif. They can be compared to the doctrine of original sin. Instead of seeing ourselves as successes here and now on this planet, instead of believing in the perfection of our bodies and minds, we are told to believe that our bodies are rotten inside, filled with "poisons" and "rubbish." Our bodies are bad; we are bad. Salvation comes through fasting.

Fast and free yourself from the "toxemia," from the filthy wastes produced by your body.

These concepts, very naïve in terms of present-day thinking, remain incredibly powerful. Time and again, intelligent people on fasts will comment on how the poisons are being released. The basic religious nature of the concepts is very appealing. When people fast under such belief-systems, the activity assumes a degree of self-fulfillment that gives power to concepts that simply will not stand up to rational scientific investigation.

The religious theme is exemplified in the following passage taken from advertising copy for *The Philosophy of Fasting: A Message to Sufferers and Sinners* by Edward Earle Purinton, a book written many years ago:

His work is the product of an enthusiast along the lines of being. He is an explorer afloat on the ocean of existence, with a ready pen to record what he sees, what he feels, what he desires, what he hopes for. His mystic sympathies give birth to an iridescent philosophy that is ballasted by a sincere effort to shed from his soul-binding flesh its pains and impurities, that he may the more readily mount the eternal palace stairs of health and truth and beauty. He has discovered a Fountain of Youth where the ailing body may wash away its pains, troubles, weakness, blindness and rise like a god refreshed and ablaze with joy and ambition. He describes this fountain in these words:

"Fasting, rightly conducted and completed, is nearest a panacea for all mortal ills of any drugless remedy I know, whether physiological, metaphysical, or inspirational. Fasting, resting, airing, bathing, exercising and hoping—these six simple measures, if sanely proportioned and administered, will cure any case of acute disease. And almost any case of chronic disease."

Mr. Purington ought to know what he is talking about, for he has actually experienced a fast of thirty days' duration, and his book is a log of his sensations. He says he "found God through this fast." His object was not merely to eliminate poisons from his body through fasting but to fast for "health, enjoyment, freedom, power, beauty, faith, courage, poise, virtue, spirituality, instinct, inspiration, and love."

One thing that seems to hold is the fact that there is very little evidence that there are any practical health benefits to be gained through fasting. If there are such benefits, they await serious documentation. Some work is now being done in the Soviet Union, using fasting as a means of aiding schizophrenics, but the research is far from conclusive. Why, then, would anyone want to fast? Here are some reasons:

(1) *Rest and Cleaning.* While the fast is not a cure for any ailment, it does slow down the metabolism of the body and provide a rest for the digestive system. During this period, the accumulated material in the intestines will be cleaned out. The body does have a regenerative function and repairs itself. By fasting, the energy which usually goes into the normal functions of the day-to-day running of the energy system, can be transferred to the self-help, self-repairing systems of the body.

(2) *Weight Reduction.* In cases of chronic obesity, a prolonged fast provides excellent health benefits. This technique can result in amazing reductions of weight and, in many cases, can be the last effective resort for people with desperate weight and health problems.

(3) *Spiritual Exercise.* People have fasted in conjunction with religious observations since recorded history began. It is still a part of most

organized and esoteric religions and definitely has a place in our culture today.

(4) *The Fasting High.* Fasting produces a different state of consciousness. You could say a "nonordinary state," but this description breaks down after a fast, during which you just might have the realization that the "normal" foodbound reality under which we operate is similarly a human-induced state, and there is nothing normal or "real" about it other than our habit of staying in it through the constant and unremitting use of food.

(5) *Self-Understanding.* Fasting is a wonderful way to learn about food, a wonderful way to learn about yourself. The most important things in our lives are always those that are invisible to us.

A good example is the great East Coast electrical blackout of 1965. Suddenly, around 6:00 P.M., the entire city of New York (as well as other sectors of the northeastern United States) went dark. There was a huge electrical failure. Street lights went off. Elevators stopped. Traffic lights went out. Homes and offices were without electricity. Hospitals shut down. The city was thrown into turmoil. Transportation, emergency services, all broke down. For the first time since the invention of electricity, we suddenly had revealed to us what it actually meant in our daily lives. By not having electricity for those brief hours, we saw it for the first time. The effect of that lesson was remarkable.

Fasting will provide the same means for understanding your relationship with food. Only by denying yourself all form of nourishment for a certain period of time, will you gain insight into your own mental and bodily relationship with food. It can be a very remarkable experience to face up to your own patterns for the first time. The way to get there is through a fast.

Supervision

There are several options concerning supervision during a fast. You can go it alone. You can work with your medical doctor. You can find some experienced fasting expert. You can got to a spa or clinic devoted to fasting.

(1) *Fasting Without Supervision.* The longest you should fast without supervision of a qualified person is anywhere from twenty-four to forty-eight hours. After twenty-four hours, acidosis begins to set in, a fairly serious condition which, if not carefully tracked, can lead to very serious complications. Don't be heroic. Don't think you know what's best for yourself. Do not do anything other than a very short fast without medical supervision.

(2) *M.D.'s vs. "Fasting Specialists."* There are many people who call themselves "Doctor" and indeed do have some kind of degree—nutritionist, Ph.D., etc. —who have set themselves up as qualified fasting experts and consultants. Such people may be counted upon to be proponents of fasting, sympathetic to it, and usually quite knowledgeable in the conduct of fasting. Their experience in conducting, in some cases, thousands of fasts, will be of benefit to a faster. On the other hand, most M.D.'s will be decidedly unsympathetic to, and uninterested in fasting. While there are increasing prescriptions of fasting for cases of chronic obesity, the idea of fasting to understand your body and mind, or for spiritual reasons, would be quickly dismissed by most M.D.'s.

Nonetheless, it would be irresponsible to recommend that anyone undertake a prolonged fast under the supervision of anyone other than an M.D. Here's the reason why: In ninety-five out of one hundred cases, an extended fast can be undertaken under the supervision of any experienced person as a guide, or even just through using a good book. Chances are that you will have a wonderful experience. In the other five cases something can and will go wrong. In such instances, your "fasting doctor" will not be able to help you. You won't need any fasting information, you will need prompt, effective medical help, and quickly. More important, you will have to know what to look for. The danger signs are mostly beneath the surface. The dogma presented in some fasting books that you should, or can safely fast until the coating on the tongue disappears, is a passport to the hospital, and not as a "fasting" patient. Daily, sophisticated tests administered by a physician will tell you and the doctor that the various possible danger areas are under control. These areas are not visible to the naked eye. Your guru, your Ph.D., your experienced friends will not be able to see them. Nonetheless, these signs are readily visible through analysis of various blood and urine tests which only a doctor is qualified to administer.

Let's face it. Most people go into fasting for the specific purpose of improving health and well-being. Why take unnecessary risks? Find a doctor who has some interest and knowledge in fasting, someone who will back you up on a decision to go on a fast and who will be available to work with you. Not just any doctor will do. Remember, the various non-medical specialists are probably wonderful, well-meaning people, very supportive and helpful. The problem is that all this is very fine when things are going well. When things go wrong, they won't necessarily be able to help you if you get yourself into trouble.

(3) *Fasting Spas.* There are numerous places throughout the world where fasting is given high priority as a health program. While the United States has few such spas, Europe has developed the state of the art to a high degree. Institutes such as the Bircher-Benner Clinic in Switzerland and the Buchinger Sanatorium for Biological Therapy in Germany have exisited for dozens of years and served thousands of people under carefully supervised programs.

Dr. Otto Buchinger is the director of the Buchinger Sanatorium in Bad Pyrmont, West Germany. In his book *About Fasting,* Dr. Buchinger outlines the following "dreadful orders, prohibitions and warnings" which from his experience are important to the proper conduct of a fast in his clinic. Whether or not one agrees with his medical conclusions, the following program reflects fasting procedures at European clinics:

(1) Conversations about illness, hard times, financial and other worrying matters as well as about meals, break the atmosphere of the healing and fasting. That is why they are to be left out among the circle of patients.

(2) The sanatorium is by tradition no enemy of radio, or TV, but only of the noise which either makes. Therefore, if the radio appears at all desirable during the remedial fasting treatment, have it on so softly it can be heard only in the patient's own room.

(3) Ignorance creates offenders. Don't forget: Read literature about fasting!

(4) A fasting establishment is not a sanatorium deluxe. All too worldly lavishness does not belong to the style of the time, still less, however, to the style of a fasting establishment.

(5) In a fasting clinic the ban on smoking for patients and visitors alike is compulsory. Throughout at least the entire period of treatment neither coffee nor alcohol in any form whatever are to be taken, for both coffee and alcohol overload the liver apart from other health disadvantages.

(6) Punctuality is politeness—unpunctuality is impoliteness!

(7) Visits to the cinema and theatre, although not forbidden, interfere with the full efficiency of the treatment—as too much conversation and diversion in general go against the spirit of the treatment.

(8) Between noon and 3 P.M. the mid-day rest is the rule in a fasting establishment. . . .

(9) The length of the treatment is determined by

the practitioner after consultation with the
patient in the light of the findings of the examination.

(10) The immediate care and supervision during
the treatment are arranged by the person in
charge of the ward, who keeps in constant
touch with the practitioner.

(11) The lectures on health education topics are a
part of the treatment like the fasting itself.
Non-attendance reduces the value of the treatment and for this the practitioner cannot be
held responsible.

(12) The first three days of fasting (particularly in
the first treatment) and the first three building
up days are often critical days. Do not go on
any long excursions or car rides at all. However, a walk may be taken, as desired, during
the treatment for at least half an hour in the
morning or afternoon.

(13) Baths: Twice a week by special request, a hot
bath (not over 100° F) is got ready by arrangement with the nurse. Swimming is not
allowed while fasting, splashing water up to
the knees only with approval.

Upon entering the Buchinger Sanatorium, the patient begins with a "fruit day," during which up to
two pounds of fresh fruit is allowed. During this day a
meeting is arranged with the doctor, who checks
through medical history. The following morning medical tests, such as blood and urine analysis and electrocardiograms, are undertaken. The total treatment lasts
for twenty-one days. After the fruit day, the patient is
given one day of "salt treatment." In the morning, an
ounce and a half of "Glauber's" salts (named after
Johann Rudolph Glauber) are administered in one and
a quarter pints of warm water. The bad taste is allevi-
ated by the addition of fruit juice, which is sipped
after the salt water has been drunk. This treatment aids

in bowel elimination, ensuring that the patient begins a fast with little or no residue in their bowels.

The fasting regimen on a daily basis consists of a daily morning enema, following by a drinking of a cup of peppermint or camomile tea. At 11:00 A.M. there is a feeding of a glass of freshly squeezed, clear fruit juice or vegetable broth. In the evening, tea or sweetened grape juice is allowed. Fresh clear water is allowed to taste, and a daily consultation with the doctor is arranged.

Another kind of spa, mainly devoted to weight reduction, is exemplified by the Cormillot Clinic, a very sophisticated Buenos Aires establishment. Their strict medical controls are under the direction of Dr. Alberto Cormillot, a South American internist. Twenty-five patients receive daily visits from members of a staff that includes internists, psychiatrists, endocrinologists, and social workers.

The dynamics of the clinic's system is first explained to new arrivals. A detailed questionnaire is then filled out by the patients, 90 percent of whom are women. The social and psychological aspects are emphasized as part of the treatment. Patients drink two quarts of liquid per day, which can be water, coffee, tea, diet soda, etc. Occasionally a glass of milk or clear broth is allowed. Dr. Cormillot points out that after twenty-four hours, acidosis may occur. At that point the patient must be under competent medical supervision, as various complications can quickly develop.

Most people stay at the clinic about a month, but some have stayed over one hundred days. The staff monitors the patient's metabolism and alters the programs as changes occur.

Some patients do spot fasting on an outpatient basis, visiting the clinic weekly. They fast two or three days a week, and in the remaining days they eat a very specific high-protein diet. The clinic is located at Lauta ro 93, Buenos Aires, Argentina.

The United States has few well-developed clinics devoted to fasting. There are various hospitals and rest homes used by doctors for fasting overweight patients. These are generally preexisting facilities of a general-purpose nature. You get into them through your doctor. Other "fasting spas" are usually run by unaccredited individuals. In one case, a well-known "clinic" near New York City was recently exposed as having a director with a somewhat dubious degree from a Ph.D. diploma mill in England.

Two English fasting establishments are Enton Hill, located in Godalming, Surrey, England, and Tyringham Naturopathic Clinic, located in a Georgian mansion halfway between London and Birmingham.

One thing to consider about the fasting clinics not specifically devoted to weight reduction is their almost religious bias towards the vocabulary and realities of the natural-health movement. In most cases, this is an evangelical and antimedical world. It is certainly not for everyone. Check out any institution very carefully. Find out who is the responsible party and make sure they have the proper credentials.

Short-Term and Long-Term Fasting

There is an interesting question as to just when a fast begins. Many people believe that just stopping the input of any form of nourishment constitutes the beginning of a fast. Thus, you wake up in the morning to break the fast: "breakfast." Others feel that the fast begins when the body uses up its immediate stores of predigested nourishment and begins to burn its own tissue for energy. If you accept the latter theory, the term "short-term fast" is a misnomer if you are talking about a period of less than three days.

Yet I happen to believe that short-term fasts are very beneficial. True, the very profound bodily and mental changes do not occur, or even begin to occur, until about the third day of a fast, but there are very strong benefits to short-term fasting.

First, there is no need for medical supervision. Nobody hurts himself or herself in a serious way by fasting for a day or two. (It goes without saying that this applies to healthy individuals. If you have any medical problems, go see your doctor before trying any kind of fast.) Short-term fasting is a great way to give your body a rest. It's a proven method of cleaning out the digestive system. There is almost a guaranteed weight loss of up to three pounds a day. It works as an aid to concentration and meditation, whether spiritual or otherwise.

In other words, you can get nearly all the benefits of a long-term fast with little of the risk and certainly a great deal less inconvenience. True, the profound bodily changes that lead to the heights of fasting euphoria are not going to happen to you in a day or two, but do not underestimate the powerful effects. They are there.

While many of the fasting practitioners of the past have recommended all kinds of plans, such as the "one meal a day" plan or the "no-breakfast" plan, if you are serious about fasting, you should bite the bullet and give up solid food for at least a period of twenty-four hours. Some fasting experts allow raw vegetable or fruit juices during fasts. The most common prescription, however, is no nourishment whatsoever, the "diet" being limited to water, unsweetened (or artificially sweetened) tea or coffee, and diet sodas.

The "rules" for conducting a fast are much the same for short- or long-term fasts, the differences being mainly in the areas of preparing for and breaking the fast. Obviously, much greater care must be taken if you are going to close down your digestive system for any great length of time. During a short fast, the digestive system is still very much in operation. Still, some care is required when breaking the fast.

Preparing for a Fast

There are many "rituals" for entering into a fast, probably forgotten leftovers from a time when fasting was an inherent form of cultural activity. One plan suggests cutting out breakfast for several days, replacing it was a glass of warm water; lunch would consist of raw vegetables and fruits; dinner would be composed of vegetables and greens. No animal protein would be allowed.

Another system proposes a raw fruit diet for at least seven days, the last three days of which are solely made up of liquids—raw fruit juices.

These preparations certainly are not going to hurt you. but you may want to keep in mind that the major preparation for a fast is not a prefast diet, but your own attitude, the environment you will inhabit, and the people with whom you will have to deal during your fast.

To start your fast, simply stop eating. There is no need for exotic rituals and diets. However, a little common sense is in order: A day or so before the fast, it might be a good idea to cut down on heavy eating and eat low-calorie meals. Cut down on the amounts eaten at every meal and avoid acid-forming foods such as meats or fish. Fresh fruits and vegetables are good to eat before a fast, since they aid in elimination.

Conducting the Fast

Water: The whole idea behind fasting is for the body to nourish itself from excess reserves. Thus, no nourishment is called for in general. This does not mean that nothing should be taken into the system. In order for the internal systems to work properly, there is always a strong need for plenty of water. You should drink about two, and as many as three, quarts of water every day. Don't force yourself if you're not thirsty, but remember to drink *at least* a full glass at every "mealtime" and also in between whenever you feel like it. Make sure that the water is not too cold, and be especially careful to avoid ice. Room temperature is best.

Water is important to avoid dehydration and to replenish the supply of water which is lost in very large amounts when the body goes into acidosis, usually in the second or third day of the fast.

The important thing to keep in mind is that during

a fast your body still uses food—the stored breakdown of foods you have already eaten. Water is a key element of the metabolic process for breaking down such foods.

Rest and Relaxation: While fasting, your metabolism slows down considerably. The calories you would normally burn from food, calories which are consumed as part of your normal activities, are no longer available. The demands the body makes on itself are great and therefore, it's best to consider your fast as a period of solitude, introspection, quiet—in effect, a period for hibernation. Quiet your emotions. Don't hassle with anyone. Don't drain your energy through anger or fear. Try to avoid negative thinking. Lie around in bed. Read. Relax. Avoid all strenuous exercise or manual labor. A brisk fifteen-to-twenty-minute walk is about all the exercise you should take. It's best to conserve as much energy as possible.

For these reasons, it's much better to be out of the city if possible, away from the daily chores and activities of your normal routine. Friends, neighbors, lovers, wives, husbands, and children can be a definite interference during this period. The best situation is one where you have your privacy and solitude and can control the amount of interpersonal contact you have with other people.

In no case should you try to conduct any kind of extended fast in situations where you are working or under stress.

Treating Bad Breath: One of the by-products of your fast will be one of the worst cases of bad breath you will perhaps ever encounter. This will usually occur during the second day and continue through the fast. Your tongue will also most likely become coated with a whitish color. Most of the earlier fasting experts attributed this bad breath to the elimination of "toxins." This is not really quite the case, unless you consider normal amounts of adipose (fatty) tissue, always necessary to your body in the right amounts, as "poisons." The bad breath is not the elimination of poisons from your body. The internal system switches over from

burning incoming foods to the use of ketone bodies
for its main source of energy. When the bodily system
goes into ketosis, one of the forms of ketone bodies,
acetone, is oxidized through the respiratory function
of the lungs. You breathe it out. That is what is responsible for the bad breath.

You can deal with this problem in several ways.
One, you don't have to consider it a problem. Bad
breath is certainly subjective, it is based on condition-
ing since childhood. Perhaps bad breath is part of the
natural fasting process and can simply be lived with.
Two, you can use toothpaste, mouthwash, etc. The fact
is that both these products contain nutritive material,
which is not widely known. They will make you pre-
sentable to the rest of the world, but you will still have
a bad taste in your mouth. However, it is probably
better to use such products, or even sugarless gum,
rather than be embarrassed to talk to anyone.

Bathing: Some fasting experts recommend that you
bathe regularly, as the system is supposedly therapeuti-
cally cleansed by the elimination of "toxins" through
the skin during a fast, and the bathing will aid in this
process. This is not the case, but you will still want
to keep clean and maintain your normal hygienic
routine during your fast.

Bathing during a fast is not a simple matter. Your
body develops postural hypotension—a greatly reduced
blood pressure. You should avoid very hot or very cold
water in baths or showers. Very often, a person will
take a very hot bath during a fast, stand up quickly,
and faint dead away or at least get dangerously dizzy.
In any event, extremes in temperature will sap your
system of much-needed energy.

Try to keep the water as close to your body temperature as possible. Wash yourself with dispatch and get
right out. This is not the proper time for the wonderful,
relaxing rituals of bathing. Don't soak in the tub. If
you are extremely weak, don't even go in the shower.
Try a sponge bath. Be particularly careful to avoid
saunas or steam rooms.

Warmth: Due to the drop in blood pressure and the slowing down of the body's metabolism in general, there is a tendency to get chilled. This affects the hands and the feet in particular. They are apt to get quite cold even during the summer. Two of these effects of being chilled are a slow-down of elimination processes and an uncomfortable feeling which will make it hard for you to get to sleep. Dress warmly, according to season. If your feet get cold, try wearing warm socks—even in the summer.

Elimination: As the digestive process stops, so does the automatic movement of the bowels, the peristaltic action. The problem, then, is how to eliminate the accumulated waste along the intestinal tract of the food you have eaten before the fast commenced. There are three options (1) do nothing, (2) take enemas, or (3) take laxatives.

Some of the more exotic prefast diets are geared to the elimination of digested foods during the first few days of a fast. For that reason, fruits and vegetables are recommended immediately before commencing a fast. Even so, there is a tendency for food to become impacted.

The "great enema debate" has been in full swing for at least fifty years. Some fasting proponents maintain that enemas should be a daily ritual, necessary at least during the first four days of a fast, and every few days after that. Rather than being habit forming, the argument goes, the enema supposedly tones up the bowels. On the other hand, other proponents recommend laxatives. Arnold Ehret, in *Rational Fasting,* recommends both enemas and laxatives.

In recent years, the medical profession has been taking a rather stern look at the use of enemas. If anything, the idea is beginning to take shape that enemas are potentially harmful and should be used most judiciously. During most hospital treatments under medical supervision, patients are given laxatives for the first few days of a fast rather than enemas.

One of the common mistakes people make when

taking an enema is to place the bag too high above them, creating water pressure so great as to injure delicate body tissue. Never hang an enema bag more than two feet above you. Better still, avoid the enema bag completely and, if you must have an enema, use the commercially prepared "Fleet" enema, which comes in a small disposable plastic container, available at all drugstores. It's much less dangerous.

A laxative is preferable to an enema. Try to use a mild natural product and stop using it after the first few days. After that, your bowels will have little to do. Let them rest.

Drugs and Fasting: The use of drugs—aspirin, alcohol, tranquilizers, marijuana, etc.—is foolish. Your body is going through the most complicated of processes, changes which are as yet to be fully charted by medical research. Ingesting any kind of drug could cause unforeseen changes which present totally unwarranted effects. Besides, in fasting, your own body works as a drug, in the most powerful sense. Leave well enough alone.

Sex and Fasting: Forget it. First of all, you probably won't want to. Second, if you want to, chances are you won't be able to. Third, you need all your energy just to keep things together for general activities. Fourth, the bad breath and coated tongue are less than attractive to you or your partner.

Face it, this is not the time for deep and meaningful personal relationships or physical contact. There's a reason the ancient faster "found God" during prolonged periods without foods. It's a very rarefied trip, and you can't take anyone else along with you.

There is a measurable drop of the male libido, or even temporary cessation, during a fast. Females have also been known to lose sexual interest during a fast. In general, do it if you want to, and if you can, but keep in mind that a fast may also be used as a period to cool it sexually for a while.

Vitamin Supplements: All the evidence is not yet in regarding vitamin and mineral losses during a fast. It is know that quantities of B6 are lost as well as abnormal amounts of potassium and sodium. A therapeutic multi-vitamin and mineral supplement are usually given on a daily basis during a fast.

Breaking the Fast

It's a poor idea to enter a fast of any length of time, other than a short-term fast, with a goal or precon-ceived notion of how long the fast will last. Complica-tions can develop, and if they do, they will be more important than any goal you have set for yourself. Fasting is not a game or a contest. Don't think of it as competition, even against yourself. You should, of course, be under a doctor's supervision for any fast lasting more than a few days. Even under a doctor's care, your first fast should not last more than a week.

Ending, or breaking the fast can be as crucial as the fast itself. Your body goes into a state of hiberna-tion during the fasting period. Your digestive processes have virtually stopped. Your stomach has shrunk. Your intestines are emptied out. You are in no way prepared for the intake of solid food. The shock to your system would be too much. Several deaths have been reported in medical journals dealing with complications in the refeeding stage. Indeed, Ehret made similar reports, one in particular in which a man died after eating potatoes.

In any event, do not wait for hunger to return before breaking your fast. Chances are it won't return, and you must "will" yourself back into eating. Some people get too weak and have to resume eating, other get too thin, still others have business or social reasons to get back into food. When, for whatever reason, you decide to break the fast, begin eating slowly and gradually. Do not eat any solid food whatsoever at first. Your stomach will not be able to digest it, and the least that will occur is severe intestinal pain. The complications usually come from the solid food's becoming com-pacted either in the intestine or the bowel.

Break your fast with liquids. Medical people recom-

mend two or three days on tea with sugar, the sugar
being a means of rapidly reversing the ketosis associated with the fast. Other fasting experts recommend
freshly squeezed, raw fruit juice. Still others follow
Ehret's dictum of breaking the fast with stewed spinach.

A rule of thumb is to stay on one day of liquids for
every three days that the fast has lasted. Drink only
half a glass or cup at first and follow with a full glass
or cup every few hours. Do not drink more than a pint
at one sitting. If you drink juices, make sure they are at
room temperature. Sip the juices slowly in order to
avoid stomach cramps.

Even after a very short fast, do not jump back into
solid foods right away, even though your digestive
processes are still working. After a one-day fast, your
stomach can handle solid foods, but they must be light.
Rich foods should be avoided.

The medical people recommend following several
days of tea with sugar with a light 300–500 calorie
diet as recommended in Chapter 5. *Fat Fasts.* In any
event, remember to do it gradually, slowly reintroducing fruit, eggs, cheese, small quantities of meat, etc.
Your stomach will have shrunk, and you will need a
smaller quantity of food.

Do not overeat. A slow caloric buildup is in order.
After the fast is broken, hunger returns with a ven-
geance. You have to maintain great self-control during
this period, which can last ten to fourteen days. It is
during this time that people who have fasted to lose
weight gain a great deal of it back. This is a refeeding
phase in which you have to reeducate your body by
reintroducing it slowly back to correct foods in
moderate amounts.

After the Fast

It is obvious that most of us do not have the opportunity to devote extended periods of time on a regular basis to prolonged fasts. What we can gain from
our fasts is a new idea of ourselves and our bodies.
Also, it is possible to extend the benefits by conducting

intermittent series of short-term fasts. Try a one-day-a-week or weekend fast. You will give yourself a rest, possibly lose weight, and get away from the time, money, and energy spent on food.

Monodiets and Partial Fasts

Rice diets, the "European Grape Cure," raw juice fasts, etc, are partial fasts. In a technical sense, either you are fasting or you are eating. There's no in-between. Even liquid juices have nourishment, and the essence of fasting metabolism is that the body sustains itself on its own internal nourishment.

Thus, monodiets or partial fasts are really just a form of diet, and a very poor one at that, since they will inevitably be unbalanced and not provide adequate nourishment.

Still, certain monodiets are useful as a prelude to fasting, the best of which consists of freshly extracted raw fruit and vegetable juices. My book *Nature's Drinks* (Vintage, 1973) supplies many recipes and the necessary information for preparing such drinks.

7

STORY OF A CONSCIOUSNESS FAST

"There is among us a sister who has been favored with wonderful gifts or revelations which she experiences in an ecstasy of the spirit during the sacred ceremonies of the Lord's Day. She converses with angels and sometimes, with the Lord Himself. She perceives hidden mysteries and has the power of reading the hearts of men and of prescribing remedies for such as need them. 'Among other things,' she reported, 'I have seen a soul in bodily shape, and a spirit appeared to me, not an empty and filmy thing, but an object which could be taken in the hands, soft and light, and of ethereal color, and in shape altogether like a human being. That was my vision.' "

—TERTULLIAN, on the fasting
Montanists of Carthage

"But thou, when thou dost fast, anoint thy head and wash thy face, so that thou mayest not be seen by men to fast, but by thy Father, who is in secret."

—JESUS

Damian, twenty-eight years old, is an advertising executive. He lives and works in New York City:

The longest I usually fast is between ten and fourteen days. I was tasting spiritualism at the time. I was very, very hungry for higher consciousness and seeking spiritual nourishment. I knew that there was something else, and I wanted to go through every door. So I was looking for things, and fasting was one of them. It was the means for me to control and turn off the carriage, my body.

During sickness we come in contact with the fact we don't want to eat, so I was aware of the fact that *eating perhaps could be a belief-system that I grew up with.* A belief that you have to eat three times a day. Whether or not it's your body telling you, it's your mind telling you. I wanted to turn off that part of me that said, "Hunger." I was also aware that there's a very subtle enjoyment in the feeling called hunger. So, I wanted to turn off that thing that said, "Eat," and I knew that I could do it, because in sickness I had experienced nausea at the sight of food after even two or three days, and upon getting better, I had almost no will at all to eat. I kept saying to myself, "I know I've got to eat because people are saying I've got to eat now, but I don't feel hungry."

I knew that there was a domain I could get into called "fasting." I didn't know how long that could last. The first fast I did was through the urging of a woman I knew. She turned me on to Arnold Ehret and his "mucousless diet." I said, "Wow, this guy is absolutely insane." I read the book he wrote and could see his mental spaces. And the mental spaces, and not information on fasting, is what I got from him. He had obviously been on a fast a little too long— that's what his book said to me. Something had burned out of him. However, he was describing some things I would later experience, which suggests to me that what I got was Arnold's "program" for fasting. In other words, what Arnold said a fast was, became what a fast is for me.

The first fast I did was for six or seven days. I initially started to fast with no idea of a time limit. I realized that after two days, my appetite was gone. I had an incredible amount of energy. I was quite surprised by that. And I could work and concentrate.

What I was doing in terms of the fast was taking citrus juices and water and tea. Also, I sometimes took coffee. I found I got a tremendous hit from the coffee. It was just like—"BOOM"—a jolt. Then I found that the jolt wasn't the same if I didn't put honey in. Also, my ability to concentrate increased with the amount of honey I had put in. It would be energy that my mind would use, it seemed, rather than my body.

I found that I went through cycles on the fast. There are periods of time in which you have a tremendous amount of energy and physical energy and you want to work out. I sometimes felt an urgent need for physical exercise during the fast. And then I would go through another period of the cycle in which I would be very lethargic and tire very easily and lose my ability to concentrate.

One problem was that while on that first fast, I didn't know what to do with it. I had all this great energy. There were nights when I just couldn't sleep, and I didn't know what to expect, because it was all new to me in terms of my own experience. During the fast I would focus on and get a tremendous "hit" off the word *fast,* it became a double-entendre that would take me from *fast,* from movement, to *fasten,* to stick to someplace. I'd be stuck in a space and it would be maybe two hours later that I realized that the rest of the world wasn't with me in that space, that I was somehow in a separate space—a different reality. And I was surprised that others weren't sharing this space. If someone else was in the room with me, I would be surprised that he was in a different space.

Operating from these levels was very interesting in terms of going to work every day in an advertising agency. The only person I told about my fast was the woman who turned me on to it in the first place. And she had never fasted. She passed the book on to me because someone had passed it on to her.

When you pick up a book for the first time, you are accepting other people's programs as to what a fast is. And your fast will become that program. It becomes self-fulfilling. If the book says that the fast will clean you out, will "detoxify" your system, you better believe that you will feel cleaned out and detoxified—whether or not there is any reality behind it. The point is that rather than reality you are accepting a belief. If you believe it, it will be as if it were true. And that's what happened when I picked up Ehret's book on fasting.

The other thing that happened is that I lost all desire for food. It wasn't a sense of "I wish I could eat now," or "Wouldn't it be nice to have a hamburger," or "Wouldn't it be nice to anything." It was interesting, because I hadn't eaten meat in a long time and I would flash on meat and get a very strange sense of what meat was. I felt something very positive about meat but also very negative about it. It was okay for people to eat meat, but it seemed very heavy, not desired in my body. On the other hand, I could almost get into a rhapsody about vegetables all of a sudden. What I found was that I was really getting into the aesthetics of what a vegetable was. But there was no hunger in terms of eating it. I could appreciate it without wanting to consume it. That was very nice.

After six or seven days, another part of me said, "Wow, it's been six days and you'd better eat," so I went out and got some spinach and steamed it, and it just went right through me, just like an express train. I felt very much cleansed. Also, I was coming back down. The feeling of food back in me brought me right down. It was as though my consciousness had expanded and the air was now coming out of the balloon and I was becoming centered once again. It brought me down and grounded me. I got tired, a feeling of weariness, and then I became very much aware of my body in terms of putting food in to consume it, and aware that food has become something sacred to me. I don't mean sacred in terms of worship—just that my body became important to me and the food that came into it became important to me. This was opposed to my previous attitude of just stuffing myself with food. I realized just how little consciousness I ever had about eating. I eat very quickly. By fasting I became aware of that. Once the first fast was over, I knew I could do it at will and use it as I use other things. In other words, it now became part of my game.

I didn't appreciate at the time what it was. I put a value on it and used it in foolish ways—the attitude of "I can fast," or "Sure, everybody should fast" kind of thing. I played "fast." "Are you fasting?" or "Why aren't you fasting?" became oneupmanship or gamesmanship at parties. I fasted and told people to fast for all the various good reasons. I used it to "use," rather than for what it is. However, it does work, in spite of the use you want to put it to. It does what it does whether you're hip to it or not. So I fasted two days out of every week, always on weekends. I would fast Saturdays and Sundays. Then I got clear that I wanted to use it differently. I became aware of what the fast could do.

Each of my fasts was different. If you go into a fast saying, "I'm going to fast for forty-eight hours," you tend to fast for forty-eight hours, and maybe another twelve, and then you have to eat. It's as though the deal up front is whatever it is and all of a sudden you find yourself in a scene where you are going to eat.

There have been some two- or three-day fasts when in the middle of the night I'll be dreaming about food. Also, there have been fasts that I broke with a pint of Häagen-Dazs ice cream. All the while I'm saying to myself that it's ridiculous to break a fast with Häagen-Dazs, but I was lusting after it so much I would say that's what I'm going to do right now. Later, I would say to myself, "What the hell did you just fast for if you're going to eat Häagen-Dazs ice cream." So you do these kind of games with yourself. You're really kidding yourself if you walk into the fast without being absolutely clear on why you're doing it, on how the fast can effect your consciousness. It does it anyway, but if you don't know about it up front, you miss a lot of the movie.

One interesting thing about the fasts I've done is the dizziness, the blackout sensation. I got to enjoy that. There are times when you are fasting, if you stand up quickly, it's absolutely mind-blowing.

I use the fast now on Mondays to get very clear. I work at an agency where I'm responsible for a significant part of their business. I would use the fast on Monday to take care of all my conceptual work so that the rest of the week was just filling it out. All the thinking and the creating I would do on Monday, and on a fast it would be very easy to get it all done with a high degree of discipline.

The fast would make me very clear-headed. If you eat lunch, you sometimes don't recognize the effect it has on the body. It's like a martini for someone who drinks. It's sluggishness—you feel the blood go out of you. After a heavy meal it takes at least two hours to clear out your head. I'm talking about major food—a dinner, a business lunch. If you eat food in that way, and I'm not even talking about drinking, just eating, it takes a tremendous amount of time. If you have a two and a half hour business lunch, you're not good until 4:00 P.M., and by that time the day is just about over.

So I would fast through the day, and it would be very easy to concentrate. The next day, after breaking the fast, I would lose that power of concentration but gain other things. It's a trade-off. So, by being aware of the cycle, I could use that part of the cycle for my own purposes. That's what it's there for.

Another part of my "program" is that I have to have fruit or vegetable juices when I fast. I read one book which said that you should only drink distilled water on a fast. This is very difficult unless you are able to lie down and sleep for long periods of time. I've tried the distilled-water approach. One big problem is to get distilled water that's not in plastic containers and thus doesn't taste like plastic. That, of course, is an immediate turn-off. For me, if I have to work, if I have to deal and interact on a professional level with people who couldn't care less whether I was fasting or eating pastrami sandwiches, then I have to be able to deal with that, and to deal with it responsibly. I provide myself with the necessary energy by drinking orange juice or tea or coffee with honey.

The following is experiential: When I'm drinking, if I just drink water, it leads to a different consciousness. I don't put any more value on it than any other, but I can't function effectively in it. But I can function in the real world by drinking citrus juices. I have a juicerator and I would have grapefruit in the morning and it would be difficult to carry it with me during the day, so I would take Tropicana, which was a tremendous lift for me.

Taste is very important in the fast. You become kind of a connoisseur of juices. Taste is greatly enhanced, and you learn to drink slowly, very slowly. I would sip and savor every drop.

The longest I've ever fasted was fourteen days, but I realized that length didn't matter. I had to will myself back to eat. I could have gone much further, and I would like to do an extended fast. As I put food back into my stomach, I could see what effect food has on me—food itself as well as additives. I know that additives make me crazy, or at least have an effect on my system that I'm sensitive to. I'm also aware that foods have the same potential. There is something very different about the effects of cabbage and eggplant. I would like to have the benefit of more professional knowledge to be able to do an extended fast, because I am aware of the potential of the will to really hurt yourself, because you can go off on a fast and realize that there is danger in it. I want a guide to take me through a long fast. I find that doctors are just the worst. They don't want to hear about fasting. This is

probably because they don't understand it. Where
they're coming from is total "not"-understanding of
why you would possibly want to go on a fast.

It's interesting, because one doctor I had gone to
for a physical said that I had high cholesterol and he
wanted me to have another special test done specifically
to check the cholesterol level. So I did the test and he
said that it was above average, but nothing extraordinary. So, I immediately said, "Okay," just like that,
and turned the whole thing right off and didn't eat
meat any more. I just got into a vegetable diet with
some cheese. I didn't eat an egg for about six months.
Then I went back for another test. He did the test and
said, "This is incredible, you have no levels now. It's
below normal." This was within a year of the first
examination. I said, "Yeah, but I stopped eating meat,
I stopped using butter, and I stopped eating eggs."
And he said, "You did all that? Why did you do it?"
It was beyond him that you would literally stop doing
the whole thing. I tried to talk to him about fasting,
but he just doesn't understand it. And yet, he is always
on a diet. Any diet to me is a kind of fast. You
don't eat all night and then you break the fast. That's
how "break-fast" got its name. It's a question of
realizing that you are fasting and that you would like
to have a little control and see what happens if you
prolong a fast.

During one of my fasts, I was pondering the idea
that man, in ancient times, when we were closer to
our animal senses, would fast for periods of time out
of necessity in terms of traveling for great periods
of time and distance. Then they would eat quite a bit,
then travel, and so on. It made sense that one would
need the ability of not eating for extended periods of
time and then really eat well when food was available.
It probably allowed early man to travel across great
spaces swiftly and with relative high energy, and to
be really clean with what they had to do. There must
be a tremendous contact high when you get a group of
people together fasting. I got a wonderful feeling off of

the National Fast Day held recently on behalf of some worthy cause. Up front I said, "What a fraud, what a bullshit thing." Then I said, "What kind of communication this must be for everybody that does fasting!" I expected some sort of communication would take place. And I felt really nice fasting that day—a tremendous sense of elation. Not an elation because we were saving somebody or something, but a high from the fast, because I was communicating with people in the same space. I felt very good, and also very sad at times. I found it very easy to weep, or to be at the verge of tears, for very little reason.

I like to be alone when I fast. I don't like to have input from other people, because usually other people aren't sensitive to the space you're in, and that's fine, but I find that for me it allowed a very personal communication. It puts you in a frame where you can communicate on other levels. You're sensitized. It allowed me to get into myself as compared to me getting into other people. Whereas, food is something it's nice to share. One sits down and wants to break bread with friends and uses that as a social medium for exchange.

So I think of a fast as literally the opposite of sitting and eating and breaking bread with someone. This goes beyond ordinary social intercourse and into sexual intercourse. In terms of sex, fasting is similar to taking drugs with sex. There are times when I can have sex that is fantastically rewarding and other times when I am incapable of having sex at all. There are times during the fast when my sexual drive is just not there. There are other times when it is very keen. It's a lot like taking speed. I took drugs for a long period of time. I had asthma as a kid, had my own adrenalin, and was tripping most of the time. What really turned me around was getting through *The Doors of Perception* by Huxley and realizing where insights really came from. The fact is that I was waltzing around at five or six years old tripping, doing speed, and wondering why, after third grade, school became something weird. Not only was I the smartest kid in the class but, more important, I realized that it all didn't matter. I was into other things besides the regular schoolwork. For instance, reading—I would pick up a book and jump into it. I would have the feeling of really being there, it was just like a movie. Fasting reminded me of drugs, particularly with regard to having sex. For instance, when I take speed, there are times when sex is a very strong drive, a very lasting desire. There are other times when the most voluptuous of partners evokes no sexual interest at all. I find the same thing to be true with fasting.

Fasting is very similar to being high. It *is* high. That's what impressed me about Ram Dass's thing, that you don't have to come down. I took that very literally. Not taking drugs, I became just the very opposite. I don't even take aspirin now. I want to feel it all myself now. And this is something that I feel people should realize, especially people who dull themselves. The body is a natural high. If you really want it to be high, you can tune it to be high.

I would like to get into a long fast so I can learn what foods do to me, or what certain foods do to me in particular. Then I could constitute a diet. One could then ingest food as one could previously ingest a drug. Instead of playing Russian roulette, you would get control over the food that's coming into the body.

I hadn't taken drugs in several years. I had been meditating with the purpose of taking mescaline which had been given to me. During a fast I took the mescaline and found that I hadn't gone anywhere. I was at the very same place. It was the same kind of realization as when Ram Dass gave the LSD to his master, his Indian guru, and the guy swallowed all he wanted to and didn't get anywhere. The mescaline altered my reality. But then I looked at myself in a mirror, started to laugh, and came right back to where I had been.

A fast is really incredible for you. As you fast, you become more and more aware that what is happening to you is not essentially what is happening to the person who is sitting across the room from you. The thing I had to learn, and what everyone who fasts will learn experientially, is that what you think in reality for everyone, is only reality for you. And it comes to you very clearly when you think you've got what everyone is talking about and then someone says to you not only did they not get it but it didn't make any sense.

I went into fasting for consciousness and that's why, if you go into it to lose weight, you'll lose weight. But there's another channel to watch, and I want everyone to be aware that whatever this channel is used for, people should know that it's there—so turn the channels and tune them. If you are going into it only to lose weight, absolutely fine. That's perfectly valid. But enjoy the show. The problem is that many people don't know how to change the channel. They can't even find the knob. The way to do it is as follows: When you get into a fasting space—and believe me, you'll know because in ordinary experience you would get into the space called "daydreaming," such as "I can't concentrate, I'm daydreaming"—all of a sudden you'll be somewhere else, totally somewhere else, and then you hear a voice talking to you and that voice is part of your expanded-consciousness daydream. If you want to call it a daydream, fine, but enjoy the daydream and know that what you're coming back to is another part of the dream. At least provide that possibility for yourself while you're fasting. Daydreaming may frighten you, because you can't concentrate and control your mind. If you do get frightened, take some honey in tea or coffee. The honey is really good for getting you centered quickly—at least it is for me. Honey will really put you back down, give you a center. It seems to go right to your brain and your brain uses it very quickly, no more than five minutes. It's a hit and you know it. And think in terms of hits too. Although I'm using drug metaphors, I do want to keep away from drugs. Fasting is something in and of itself. We can talk about drugs to help explain how we feel during a fast, but it is really using the fine tuning of the body as a drug in itself. I plan to keep away from drugs.

Fasting is important to me because it expands my consciousness and hopefully improves the world I live in. Fasting can be important for drug-oriented people, people who are interested in getting high and looking at channels, being aware of these channels, and using them. It's also important for people who are not oriented toward drugs to be able to take a fast for various purposes—among them, to lose weight. It's a very effective way to lose weight for that special moment when you want to fit into your clothes. You can lose a lot of weight very quickly.

Fasting is very definitely a non-ordinary state of reality in the Don Juan-Carlos Castaneda sense, but it's hard to say "non-ordinary state of reality" after you've fasted. The realization you get after the fast is that there are no "ordinary" states of reality. A fast can put you in contact with that insight—if you let it; if you get out of the way of your mind. The reality that "this is where we are now" is controlled by the centering of the food we eat. Take food as a drug. Just consider the food you are ingesting as a means of keeping you "here." Right where I am now. In eating, imagine it as a drug, keeping you on this level. Do not eat and watch the different level you are at, or eat different foods and watch the levels. You're ingesting something into your system. Think of food as energy. Different foods are different kinds of energy. It's energy that changes your head. What you do with that energy, that food, is to reach certain mental levels. Also, you can allow your body to live off its own stored energy and reach the fasting space.

After you fast, there's a period of time when you don't lose weight after a while. I used to be around 190, and then I stopped eating meat and dropped to around 175. Then, when I started fasting, I got to around 160. I've held that 160 now for quite a long time. I've also noticed that I eat quite a bit less than I did before fasting. The desire to eat a lot, to consume a lot, is no longer there. I believe this is because the fear of not eating is gone. The surprising thing for me is that you eat a lot because you are afraid of what will happen to you if you don't get anything to eat. So you get through the fear of not having enough to eat. I didn't even know I was afraid of it.

One thing to remember is that the purpose of the fast generally becomes self-fulfilling. Your goals have a way of becoming realized. Also, the first three days are the most important part of the fast. You can almost feel when the turn-around comes. It is subtle, but it is very real. You then know you're fasting. You know when the first part of the fast is over. There are cycles within it.

As I said, I'm very interested in extending a fast, but only with more information and a competent guide. From a consciousness point of view you begin to realize that the different cycles are subtle mental regions. I want to know what these spaces are from my body's point of view, to plot and record what they are and when they happen. I think a medical doctor is necessary for this task, and I hope I can find one to work with me. A lot of these cycles are measurable only through medical tests. You can only go so far on personal observation. Blood levels, urine tests, metabolism, all require sophisticated medical technology. Then you can read the numbers during the fast and correlate observable phenomena with the numbers and your mental spaces. You can create your own map or guide to various levels of consciousness. The thing that is really clear to me is that where we are "now" is a space that is controlled by the ingesting of food. Food power. Food is something very special. What food is—is what keeps us at this level—in the "now"; in "reality." The awareness of food as a drug is one that is very new to me. It is a drug. It induces a state of reality which we are prone to call real, simply because this is where we are at. The fact is that the bind is reversed, that you go into an internal system during a fast which allows for another, and as valid, a reality which is virtually uncharted. It's no accident that Jesus and Moses went into the desert and fasted for extended periods, such as forty days. They would come back gleaming, having in fact visited a space that is very real where there are gods, and insights, and holiness, and enlightenment.

What it all means to me is that whereas I used to think of myself solely as a "sender," I now recognize the vast powers of my own body in molding my consciousness and I am now prone to think of myself more as a receiver. Fasting has allowed me to tune into myself better and in more subtle ways. I have a tuning fork sensation, I receive all things with the totality of my total consciousness, body, and mind.

8

THE FASTING RESORT

UNLIKE THE HOSPITAL *fast, or medically supervised clinic fast, the "fasting resort" is more often than not merely a nice quiet place to rest and fast. Most of the fasting resorts are run with no medical supervision and offer little more than room, board, and the company of fellow fasters. Still, for many people, this works just fine: a country setting, fresh air—and no food.*

The following account is by Danny, a slender, attractive Australian artist who now lives in New York City with her young son:

R. D. Laing says that there can come a point in your life when the people that you normally deal with—let's say that there are thirty people in your life—all start to reject you. It gradually gets to the point when even your closest relatives reject you, because they can't cope with you, and you can't cope with yourself. And so you are committed to a place, or you commit yourself, and the state you are in is then diagnosed as schizophrenia.

It wasn't that in my case, but it's analogous. I was too fat for myself and too fat for the people around me, so I committed myself to a fat farm. I was really just getting too heavy, but I like to jump things a bit if I feel something's inevitable. Over a period of eighteen months I had been gaining a pound or two at a time until I was about fifteen pounds overweight. And although I have a large frame, I was used to having no excess weight at all, and I feel better that way because I'm lighter and I can go faster. I chose fasting because dieting is ridiculous. You get cranky. I like to cook and I found that to eat little bits of foods is worse than eating no food at all. It's heavier on the head.

I read about this place in the New York *Times,* and it sounded perfect to me. I was interested in the idea of having no food at all, and just drinking water. And the absence of cigarette smoking appealed to me, because I smoke so much. I thought maybe that would work: cold turkey. It didn't matter to me at all that the guy who ran the place wasn't a medical doctor. All my experience with doctors had been, "Go home and take an aspirin and that will be ten dollars, please." I also thought I might get high from it, that it might be an experience. It was the ideal place for me because it was so spartan and it was out of the city and away from my immediate circumstances. Having a kid around can sometimes drive you to bagels.

So I made a reservation at this place. It's run on a first come, first served basis, and it is the price of a cheap hotel, $126 a week and no extras, because there are no extras. You are paying for water and a bed, in a big, quite pleasant house. People share bedrooms, or you can get a motel unit in the back if you want to be alone.

I got there about lunchtime on Sunday, after having a last meal of bacon and eggs and bagels and cigarettes. When I got on the train that morning with my suitcase full of clothes that didn't fit me, I thought of the shame of it if I couldn't stand it, because I had primed myself for the trip. I was more worried about cigarettes than anything else. Someone gave me a lift from the station to the place, about forty minutes outside of New York City, and I left him my cigarettes.

I checked in and was given a bed in a small room that I shared with another woman. I was given a plastic pitcher of water, and that was it. I said, "What do I do now?" and they said "Just rest." That was it. No talk of money. No talk of pulses or health. Nothing. They change your water twice a day, and that's it.

By the end of the first day I was starving, feeling hunger pangs, feeling shut in. I went to sleep and got up the next morning to weigh myself—you tend to wake up very early when you're fasting—and I was shocked and horrified because I hadn't weighed myself for a while. Then I went back to my room. Basically for the next four or five days I just slept, and every time I woke up I just put a book in front of me. I felt horrible. I truly felt horrible. It it had just been a matter of my wanting to get high or clean out my body, I think I would have left, but because I wanted to lose weight, I stayed there. The things I felt the worst about were cigarettes and coffee. For the first four days, that's all I wanted. My roommate kept popping in and out, going for drives, and so I finally asked her to get me a pack of cigarettes. By this time I could go for two hours and hardly notice it, but then I'd crave nicotine. She got them for me, and I took a walk outside the grounds and lit a cigarette. It tasted like the first cigarette I ever had. It tasted horrible, and that made me feel rather good. I put it out and went back to my room for more reading and sleeping. And every day I'd go out and test myself with a cigarette. Each time it tasted vile and horrible. I think I forgot about the food.

I really only had one high point. I guess it was about the sixth day. There are little summer houses on the grounds, and it was winter and there was snow on the ground and a frozen pond. And I sat there. I wasn't doing anything else. I had nowhere to go, nothing pressing on me. I had just done my cigarette tryout, which was disgusting. So I sat there and stared at the ice, and I felt very good, as good as I have ever felt, for just a few minutes. My mind wasn't wandering. I felt very nice, indeed.

Eventually I got a bit more social, watched a little bit of television, played backgammon. On the seventh or eighth morning I was brought a glass of orange juice. But I didn't know what the trick was—once you have a bit of food they take away your water, so you're eating, but you're thirsty. The theory is if you eat and drink together it works like blotting paper that gets wet. The liquid in you absorbs the food and it just stays together, rather than the food passing through. So I had a glass of orange juice on that divine morning, and I was really weighed down by it. I had gotten into a different body perspective.

The director assembled a couple of meetings, one of which I went to, the second of which I climbed out the window because it was so silly. At the one I went to, he introduced the house psychiatrist, a nice, friendly family-type psychiatrist, who was overweight himself. He just gave us a nice, friendly chat about how much better it was to have one glass of beer instead of four. And the director, who said he wasn't a doctor but a Ph.D., gave his pitch, mostly instructions about what to do while you're there. His main thing was rest. Don't push yourself, or go for long walks, or be too active while you're fasting, particularly in the beginning. When you stop eating, the body has no food processes to go through so the quieter you are, the more work your body can do to flush out the system. He also said, "Don't be afraid if you throw up because that will be low-grade bile," which I thought was a wonderful term. About the fifth day, I threw up and after that I felt terrific. I lost two pounds every day. I felt weak for the first five days but I didn't feel as if I was going to die—didn't feel ill or have heart flutters.

There is a staff to clean the rooms and make your bed everyday and cheer you up, and when you are eating, they serve you your food. The food is simple, but it is absolutely fresh and served in a very attractive way. The place is very well run, very efficient. There's no procedure of going in and having a day of tests. I knew well enough that if I was going to fast for ten days that I'd better check out my blood pressure and everything else before I went, so I had a physical. If I had had heart flutters, I would have said, "Take me to the nearest hospital." I think that's the most efficient way of doing it. There are no gimmicks or tricks at all. There was a TV and a gym with a few machines in it. Other than having your pulse checked every day, nothing else medical is done. No one got sick when I was there. It's left up to you. Some people who were fasting would go into the kitchen and say, "I need an orange as a pick-me-up." I guess they do that if they start to feel too sick.

All the time I was fasting I knew that I would get a coated tongue. Your breath gets weird. It smells bad and your teeth keep coating up. I cleaned my teeth about three times a day when I had the energy. I ate on the eighth and ninth days. The food consisted of orange juice, one baked apple with nothing added to it, and green salads—very simple, with lettuce, tomato, green pepper, and a little celery. It all tasted superb. They served me a baked potato just before I left, but I only ate a bit of it. I didn't want to finish it. It was delicious however, just plain.

There is supposed to be a natural end to a fast, when your body takes itself out of it, and your tongue decoats by itself. Well, I obviously interrupted myself. I fasted for an arbitrary number of days, I lost the amount of weight I wanted to lose, and I was only too glad to get out and get back to the real world. On the way back in the train, I sat in a nonsmoking car and didn't feel the need to smoke at all. But my eyes felt weird, as if they were coated with some sort of glaze, and my tongue was still coated. I was eating again, but I was still inside the fast. When I got back, people said I looked fresher and my skin seemed smoother. I was definitely thinner, but I was also definitely still in the middle of some process, because during the next couple of days my eyes felt weird and my teeth still were coated.

The first thing I wanted to do when I got back was taste white wine, because I like it. It tasted excessive, to say the least. I could taste the sugar in it. It seemed to be the richest thing in the world. I had some raw fish, which I enjoyed. I also had tempura, and that was beyond the limit. It was too rich for me to digest. I got straight back into coffee again, and after the next two or three days, I stopped noticing these things, and my body geared itself back to all the poisons—coffee, alcohol and cigarettes.

I started to gain weight almost instantly. After a week, I was five pounds heavier. I was being very careful and watching what I was eating. I found that after I hit the five-pound mark, the weight started to go again and I got to be five pounds lighter than when I came out of the place. My skin semed very loose right after I got back—similar to when I had a baby, though not as extreme—but that disappeared gradually. I do a lot of exercise, and that might be part of the reason.

I was pretty converted by the time I left to the idea of a fast being a healthy thing to do. Even if I didn't get very high in my head, or think many noble thoughts —most of the time I thought about wanting a cigarette —I did feel good when I got back. I felt cleaned out and probably a bit higher than usual. I think it's a good way to lose weight rather than torturing everyone around you by trying to eat a different sort of diet. And I would go back again, and this time try to see if, instead of thinking, "Oh, my God I can't stand it," I could be a little more constructive and not feel so depressed about the deprivations.

9

IF YOU ARE GOING TO FAST...

THIS SECTION IS intended as a quick summary of information and do's and dont's for the reader who has decided to undertake a fast.

Reasons for Fasting
(1) Rest and cleaning; (2) Weight reduction; (3) Spiritual exercise; (4) The fasting high; (5) Self-understanding.

Who Should Not Fast
People with the following ailments must not fast: (1) Diabetes Mellitus; (2) Liver problems; (3) Poor kidney function; (4) Heart disease; (5) Psychiatric disorders. People under sixteen or over fifty-five should not fast for extended periods of time, nor should pregnant women.

How Long Should You Fast?
The full effects of the fast do not begin until the second or third day, when the glycogen (carbohydrate) stores of the body are used up. Anyone in good health is relatively safe in fasting during this period. Beyond

this point, medical supervision is indicated. The fast can last as long as individual strength and good health permit.

How to Prepare for the Fast

(1) Prior to the fast, cut down on heavy eating. Eat low-calorie meals. Avoid acid-forming foods such as meat and fish. Raw, fresh fruits are excellent; they aid in elimination during early stages of the fast.

Rules for the Fast

(1) Drink two to three quarts of water a day.

(2) Rest. Relax. Avoid manual labor. Limit your exercise to brisk twenty-minute walks every day.

(3) Seclude yourself. Get out of the city. Leave your family, friends, business associates, and telephone behind. Get inside yourself and carefully control your interpersonal contact.

(4) Use a mouthwash or sugarless chewing gum to aid in controlling the inevitable bad breath associated with the fast.

(5) Bathe regularly but be careful to avoid very hot or cold water in baths or showers. Keep water as close to body temperature as possible. Avoid saunas and steam rooms.

(6) Keep warm. Don't be afraid to wear warm clothes in the summer.

(7) If bowel movements are sluggish during the first few days, use a mild, natural laxative. Discontinue after the first few days and give your bowels a rest.

(8) Do not use any drugs. This includes aspirin, alcohol, tranquilizers, marijuana, and hallu-cinogenic drugs.

(9) Limit, or avoid, sexual activities.

(10) Take a daily therapeutic multivitamin and mineral supplement.

(11) Check with your doctor before undertaking anything more than a two-day fast. Maintain

careful medical supervision for fast of extended periods.

How to Break the Fast

(1) For a short-term fast (one or two days): Break the fast with liquids or a very light, low-calorie meal of bland, cooked foods. (2) For a long-term fast: Break the fast by drinking tea with sugar. Stay one day on liquids for every three days that the fast has lasted. Drink only half a glass at first and gradually build up to a full glass every four hours. After this period of liquid feeding, begin eating meals of severely limited caloric intake. Once refeeding begins, hunger returns, which may very well be insatiable. Resist the temptations and build back up to your normal levels in very slow steps.

The ancients fasted to gain spiritual powers, to sanctify the body, to understand the nature of hidden things, to find God. The reasons for your fast may not be quite so exotic. You may fast to "clean out" your system, to rest your internal body, to shed unwanted pounds, or to gain spiritual insight. Whatever the reason, fasting will bring you in touch with your "nonfood consciousness" and provide lasting mental and physical rewards.

GLOSSARY

acetoacetic acid: A ketone body formed from excess fatty acids. Appears in the urine in abnormal amounts during fasting.

acetone: Certain substances related to acetone. Example is acetoacetic acid. Synonym for ketone body.

acetylcoenzyme A: A crucial component in fasting metabolism. Serves in the synthesis of acetoacetic acid and beta-hydroxybutyric acid, which are collectively referred to as ketone bodies. Abbreviated acetyl-CoA, or AcoA.

acidosis: A pathological condition resulting from accumulation of acid in, or loss of base from, the body. *Metabolic acidosis* is an acidosis resulting in an increase of acids other than carbonic acid. It is often caused by the ketosis or dehydration of fasting.

adipose: Of a fatty nature; fatty; fat. The fat present in the cells of adipose tissues.

aldesterone: Hormone produced in the adrenal cortex. It is very active in functions relating to the regulation of metabolism of sodium chloride, and potassium.

amino acids: Components of the chief structure of proteins; several are essential for human nutrition.

anabolism: Any constructive process by which simple substances are converted by living cells into more complex compounds, especially into living matter.

anorexia: Lack of appetite. Not to be confused with *anorexia nervosa,* a psychological disease involving the inability to eat.

basal metabolism: The minimal energy expended for the maintenance of respiration, circulation, peristalsis, muscle tonus, body temperature, glandular activity, and other vegetative functions of the body. The rate of basal metabolism (basal metabolic rate) is measured by means of a calorimeter, in a subject at absolute rest, fourteen to eighteen hours after eating, and is expressed in calories per square meter of body surface.

beta-hydroxybutyric acid: One of the ketone bodies, occurring in the urine during fasting due to incomplete fatty acid oxidation.

blood CO_2: The concentration of carbon dioxide in the blood. A high level indicates the condition of acidosis.

calorie: Unit of heat used in metabolic studies, being the amount of heat required to raise the temperature of one kilogram of water one degree centigrade.

carbohydrate: An aldehyde or ketone derivative of a polyhydric alcohol. They are so named because the hydrogen and oxygen are usually in proportion to form water. The most important carbohydrates are the starches, sugars, and celluloses.

catabolism: Any destructive process by which complex substances are converted by living cells into more simple compounds.

chloride: A salt of hydrochloric acid.

dehydrogenase: An enzyme which catalyzes the oxidation of a specific substance, causing it to give up its hydrogen.

diabetes mellitus: "Diabetes" is a general term referring to disorders characterized by excessive urine disorders. "Diabetes mellitus" is a metabolic disorder in which the ability to oxidize carbohydrates is more or less completely lost, usually due to faulty pancreatic activity, and consequent disturbance of normal insulin mechanism. This produces hypoglycemia, which produces symptoms of thirst, hunger, and weakness, and also imperfect combustion of fats with resulting acidosis.

edema: A condition in which the body tissues contain an excessive amount of tissue fluid.

electrolyte: Substance that dissociates into ions when fused or in solution, and thus becomes capable of conducting electricity.

enzyme: A protein, capable of accelerating or producing by catalytic action some change in a substrate for which it is often specific.

fasting hypoglycemia: Hypoglycemia occurring in the fasting state: after the glucose contents of the intestine have been absorbed. It occurs in such conditions as glycogen storage disease and fasting.

fat: Adipose tissue; a white or yellowish tissue which forms soft pads between various organs of the body, serves to smooth and round out bodily contours, and furnishes a reserve supply of energy.

gluconeogenesis: The formation of carbohydrates from molecules which are not themselves carbohydrates, as amino acids, fatty acids, or related molecules.

glucose: Occurring in certain foodstuffs, especially fruits and in normal blood; it is a principal source of energy for living organisms.

glucose tolerance test: Done by giving a certain unit of glucose orally or intravenously. Blood supplies are drawn at specific intervals and the blood glucose levels determined in each sample. By this means, the ability of the patient to metabolize glucose can be determined.

glycogen: The form in which carbohydrate is stored in the body for further conversion into sugar, and for subsequent use in performing muscular work or liberating heat. It is formed from sugar and part of the fat and protein in the blood, and converted when needed by the tissues into glucose.

gout: Arthritic condition caused by increased uric acid from the blood.

growth hormone: A substance that stimulates growth, especially one secreted by the anterior pituitary, which exerts a direct effect on protein, carbohydrate, and lipid metabolism and controls the rate of skeletal and visceral growth.

hepatic: Pertaining to the liver.

hormone: A chemical substance, produced in the body by an organ or cells of an organ which has a specific regulatory effect on the activity of a certain organ. Originally applied to substances secreted by various endocrine glands and transported in the blood stream to the target organ on which their effect was produced, the term was later applied to various substances not produced by special glands but having similar action.

hunger diabetes: A diabeteslike state which is characterized by decreased glucose utilization and ketosis.

hypotension: Abnormally low blood pressure; seen in shock but not necessarily indicative of it.

hyperuricemia: Excess of uric acid in the blood.

hypoglycemia: Abnormally diminished content of glucose in the blood, which may lead to cold sweat, headache, accompanied by confusion, hallucinations, bizarre behavior, and ultimately convulsions and coma.

hypohydration: State of decreased water content in the blood.

insulin: A protein hormone formed by the beta cells of the islands of Langerhans in the pancreas and secreted into the blood, where it regulates carbohydrate, lipid, and amino-acid metabolism.

ketogenic: Forming or capable of being converted into ketone bodies. Metabolic sources are fatty acids and some of the amino acids of protein.

ketogenic diet: One that produces acetone or ketone bodies or mild acidosis. This is accomplished by providing a diet wherein the ratio for fatty acid to available carbohydrates is 3 to 1 to 4 to 1.

ketone bodies: The substances acetone, acetoacetic acid, and beta-hydroxybutyric acid. Except for acetone (which may arise spontaneously from acetoacetic acid), they are normal metabolic products of lipid metabolism via acetylcoenzyme A within the liver, and are oxidized by the muscles. Acetoacetic acid is convertible to fatty acids and to steroids. Excessive production leads to urinary excretion of these bodies, as in diabetes mellitus. Ketone bodies are also sometimes known as acetone bodies.

ketonuria: Ketone bodies in the urine.

ketosis: A condition characterized by an abnormally elevated concentration of ketone bodies in the body tissues and fluids. It is a complication in diabetes mellitus and fasting.

lipid: Any of a group of organic substances which are insoluble in water, but soluble in alcohol, ether, chloroform, and other fat solvents that have a greasy feel. The lipids, which are easily stored in the body, serve as a source of fuel and are an important constituent of cell structure, and phosphatides.

lipogenesis: The formation of fat; the transformation of nonfat food materials into body fat.

metabolism: The sum of all the physical and chemical processes by which living organized substance is produced and maintained (anabolism), and also the transformation by which energy is made available for the uses of the organism (catabolism).

natriuresis: The excretion of abnormal amounts of sodium in the urine.

oxidation: Consists chemically of the increase of positive charges on an atom or the loss of negative charges. Most biological oxidations are accomplished by the removal of a pair of hydrogen atoms (dehydrogenation) from a molecule; the process of a substance combining with oxygen.

peristalsis: The wormlike movement by which the alimentary canal or other tubular organs provided with both longitudinal and circular muscle fibers propel their contents. It consists of a wave of contraction passing along the tube for variable distances.

pH: Acid-base balance.

potassium: A metallic element of the alkali group, many of whose salts are used in medicine.

protein: Any one of a group of complex organic nitrogenous compounds, widely distributed in plants and animals. Proteins, which are the principal constituents of the cell protoplasm, are essentially combinations of amino acids.

renal: Pertaining to the kidney.

sodium: A soft, silver white, alkaline metallic element; involved in the conservation of extracellular body fluid.

starvation acidosis: A variety of metabolic acidosis produced by accumulation of ketone bodies, which may accompany a caloric deficit.

systole: The contraction of the heart.

triglyceride: A combination of glycerol with the three fatty acids (steoric, aleic, and tolmitic). Most fats are triglyceride.

urea: A white, crystallizable substance found in the urine, blood and lymph. It is the chief nitrogenous constituent of the urine, and the chief nitrogenous endproduct of the metabolism of proteins. It is formed in the liver from amino acids and from compounds of ammonia.

uric acid: A crystallizable acid from the urine. One of the products of nuclein metabolism. It is nearly insoluble in water or alcohol, but soluble in solutions of alkaline salts. It also causes morbid symptoms in the blood.

BIBLIOGRAPHY

Books

Arbessman, Rudolph. "Fasting in Pagan and Christian Antiquity." *Traditio,* Vol. 7, 1949–51. New York: Fordham University Press.

Bragg, P. C. *The Miracle of Fasting.* Santa Ana: Health Science, 1973.

Brodsky, G. *From Eden to Aquarius—The Book of Natural Healing.* New York: Bantam Books, 1974.

Buchinger, O. H. *Everything You Want to Know about Fasting.* New York: Pyramid Books, 1961.

Carrington, H. *Vitality, Fasting and Nutrition.* Mokelumne Hill California: Health Research, 1963 (reprint).

Ehret, A. *Rational Fasting.* Beaumont, California: Ehret Literature Publishing, 1965.

Gregory, D. *Dick Gregory's Natural Diet for Folks Who Eat.* New York: Harper & Row, 1973.

Hazzard, L. B. *Scientific Fasting.* Mokelumne Hill, California: Health Research, 1963 (reprint).

Keys, A., Brozek, J., Henschel, A. Mickelson, O. and Taylor H. L. *Human Starvation.* Minneapolis: University of Minnesota Press, 1951.

Kunz-Bircher, R., Bircher, R. Kunz-Bircher, A., and Liechti-Von Brosch, D. *Eating Your Way to Health.* Baltimore: Penguin Books, 1972.

Lamb, L. *Metabolics.* New York: Harper & Row, 1974.

Lilliston, L. *Mega-Vitamins: A New Key to Health.* Greenwich, Conn.: Fawcett Publications, 1975.

Musurillo, Herbert. "The Problem of Ascetical Fasting in the Greek Patristic Writers." New York: Fordham University Press, 1956.

Null, G. *Biofeedback, Fasting and Meditation.* New York: Pyramid Books, 1974.

Ross, S. *Nature's Drinks.* New York: Vintage Books, 1973.

Shelton, H. M. *Fasting Can Save Your Life.* Chicago: Natural Hygiene Press, 1964.

Sinclair, U. *The Fasting Cure.* Mokelumne Hill, California: Health Research, 1923.

Wade, C. *Health Secrets from the Orient.* Englewood Cliffs, N.J.: Parker Publishing Co., 1973.

Wade, C. *The Natural Way to Health through Controlled Fasting.* New York: Arc Books, 1968.

Wagtendock, K. *Fasting in the Koran,* Leiden: E. J. Brill, 1968.

Articles

Ball, M. F., Canary, J. J., and Kyle, L. H. "Comparative Effects of Caloric Restriction and Total Starvation on Body Composition in Obesity." *Ann. Inter. Med.* 67: (1967) 60.

Benedict, F. G. "A Study of Prolonged Fasting." Carnegie Inst. Wash. Publ. no. 280, Washington, D.C., 1915.

Benoit, F. L., Martin, R. L., and Watten, R. H. "Changes in Body Composition During Weight Reduction in Obesity." *Ann. Inter. Med.* 63: (1965) 604.

Bloom, W. L. "Fasting as an Introduction to the Treatment of Obesity." *Metabolism* 8: (1959) 214.

Bloom, W. L., Azar, G., Clark, J., and Mackay, J. H. "Comparison of Metabolic Changes in Fasting Obese and Lean Patients." *Ann. N.Y. Acad. Sci.* 131: (1965) 623.

Cahill, G. F., Owen, I. I., and Morgan, A. P. "The Consumption of Fuels During Prolonged Starvation." *Advanc. Enzymol.* 6: (1968) 143.

Cheifetz, P. N. "Uric Acid Excretion and Ketosis in Fasting." *Metabolism* 14: (1964) 1267.

Consolazio, C. F., Matoush, L. O., Johnson, H. L., Krzywicki, H. J., Isaac, G. J., and Witt, N. F. "Metabolic Aspects of Calorie Restriction: Hypohydration Effects on Body Weight and Blood Parameters." *Amer. J. Clin. Nutr.* 21: (1968) 793.

————, "Metabolic Aspects of Calorie Restriction: Nitrogen and Mineral Balances and Vitamin Excretion." 21: 803.

Consolazio, C. F., Matoush, L. O., Johnson, H. L., Nelson, R. A., and Krywicki, H. J. "Metabolic Aspects of Acute Starvation in Normal Humans (10 Days)." *Amer. J. Clin. Nutr.* 20: (1967) 672.

Consolazio, C. F., Nelson, R. A., Johnson, H. L., Matoush, L. O., Krzywicki, H. J., and Isaac, G. J. "Metabolic Aspects of Acute Starvation in Normal Humans: Performance and Cardiovascular Evolution." *Amer. J. Clin. Nutr.* 20: (1967) 684.

Crumpton, E., Wine, D. B., and Drenick, E. J. "Starvation: Stress or Satisfaction?" *J. Amer. Med Ass.* 196: (1966) 108.

Drenick, E. J. "Weight Reduction by Prolonged Fasting." *Med. Times* 100: (1972) 209.

Drenick, E. J., and Blahd, W. H. "Potassium Supplementation During Fasting for Obesity." *Nutr. Rev.* 28: (1970) 177.

Drenick, E. J., Blahd, W. H., Singer, F. R., and Lederer, M. "Body Potassium Content in Obese

Subjects and Potassium Depletion During Prolonged Fasting." *Amer. J. Clin. Nutr.* 18: (1966) 278.

Drenick, E. J., and Smith, R. "Weight Reduction by Prolonged Fasting." *Postgrad. Med.* 12: (1964) A-95.

Drenick, E. J., Swendseid, M. E., Blahd, W. H., and Tuttle, S. W. "Prolonged Starvation as Treatment for Severe Obesity." *J. Amer. Med. Ass.* 187: (1964) 100.

Duncan, G. G., Duncan, T. C., Schless, C. L., and Cristofori, F. G. "Contraindications and Therapeutic Results of Fasting in Obese Patients." *Ann. N.Y. Acad. Sci.* 131: (1965) 632.

Duncan, G. G., Jensen, W. K., Fraser, R. I., and Cristofori, G. F. "Correction and Control of Intractable Obesity." *J. Amer. Med. Ass.* 181: (1962) 309.

Felig, P., Mariliss, E., Owen, O. E., Cahill, G. F., Jr. "Blood Glucose and Gluconeogenesis in Fasting Man." *Arch. Intern. Med.* 123: (1969) 293.

Foster, D. W. "Studies in the Ketosis of Fasting." *J. Clin. Invest.* 46: (1967) 1283.

Genuth, S. M. "Effects of Prolonged Fasting on Insulin Secretion." *Diabetes* 15: (1966) 798.

Harrison, M. J., and Harden, R. M. "The Long-Term Value of Fasting in the Treatment of Obesity." *Lancet* 2: (1966) 1340.

Hunscher, M. A. "A Posthospitalization Study of Patients Treated for Obesity by a Total Fast Regimen." *Metabolism* 15: (1966) 383.

Kahn, H. A. "Change in Serum Cholesterol Associated with Changes in the United States Civilian Diet, 1909–1965." *Amer. J. Clin. Nutr.* 23: (1970) 879.

Krzywicki, H. J., Consolazio, C. F., Matoush, L. O., and Johnson, H. L. "Metabolic Aspects of Complete Starvation." *Amer. J. Clin. Nutr.* 21: (1968) 87.

Maagoe, H., and Mogenses, E. F. "The Effect of Treatment on Obesity. *Dan Med. Bull.* 17: 206.

MacCuish, A. C., Munro, J. F., and Duncan, L. J. P.

"Follow-Up Study of Refractory Obesity Treated by Fasting." *Brit. Med. J.* 1: (1968) 91.

Mahler, R. J., and Szabo, O. "Studies in the Mechanism of Carbohydrate Intolerance Produced by Fasting." *Metabolism* 19: (1970) 271.

Misbin, R. T., Edgar, P. J., Lockwood, D. H. "Adrenergic Regulation of Insulin Secretion During Fasting in Normal Subjects." *Diabetes* 19: (1970) 493.

Munro, J. F., and Duncan, L. J. P. "Fasting in the Treatment of Obesity." *Practitioner* 208: (1972) 493.

Owen, O. E., Morgan, A. P., Kemp, H. G., Sullivan, J. M., Herrera, M. G., and Cahill, G. F. "Brain Metabolism During Fasting." *J. Clin. Invest.* 46: (1967) 1589.

Rooth, G., and Carlstrom, S. "Therapeutic Fasting." *Acta. Med. Scand.* 187: (1970) 455.

Runcie, J., and Thompson, T. J. "Prolonged Starvation —A Dangerous Procedure?" *Brit. Med. J.* 3: (1970) 432.

Schless, C. L., and Duncan, G. G. "The Beneficial Effect of Intermittent Total Fasts on the Glucose Tolerance in Obese Diabetic Patients." *Metabolism* 15: (1966) 98.

Smith, A. "Induction of Brain D (—) B-Hydroxybutyrate Dehydrogenase Activity by Fasting." *Science* 63: (1964) 79.

Smith, A. L., Satterthwaite, H. S., Sokoloff, L. "Induction of Brain D(—) -B-Hydroxybutyric Dehydrogenese Activity by Fasting." (1959): *Science* 163 3 January 1969: 79.

Spencer, I. O. B. "Death During Therapeutic Starvation for Obesity." *Lancet* 2: (1968) 1288.

Stinebaugh, B. J., and Schloeder, F. X. "Studies on the Natriuresis of Fasting." *Metabolism* 15: (1966) 828.

Vinyard, E., Joven, C. B., Swendseid, M. E., and Drenick, E. J. "Vitamin B6 Nutriture Studied in Obese Subjects During Eight Weeks of Starvation." *Amer. J. Clin. Nutr.* 20: (1967) 317.

Veverbrants, E., and Arky, R. A. "Effects of Fasting and Refeeding." *J. Clin. Nutr.* 20: (1969) 317.

Verdy, M., and Champlain, J. "Fasting in Obese Females." *Canad. Med. Ass. J.* 98: (1968) 1034.

Weinsier, R. L. "Fasting—A Review with Emphasis on the Electrolytes." *Amer. J. Med.* 50: (1971) 233.

NONFICTION BESTSELLERS
from
BB
BALLANTINE BOOKS

▼ Available at your local bookstore or mail the coupon below ▼